A TRUST WALK

To Gentry,
Best Wishes,
Paula King

A TRUST WALK
Mindful Golf

by Dr. Paula King
Sports Psychologist

Inkwell Productions

ISBN 0-9658158-7-0

Published By
INKWELL PRODUCTIONS
3370 N. Hayden Rd. # 123-276
Tel: 480-315-9636
Fax: 480-315-9641
Toll Free: 1-800-214-3550

Edited by:
Patricia Turpin

Typesetting Design:
Madalyn Johnson, Type 'n Graphics

Cover Design:
Thomas G. Treiber

Dedicated with love and gratitude to
Tommy

Acknowledgements

Where golf is a solitary achievement, writing a book requires a cooperative team effort to score well. I am fortunate to be part of such a team: Inkwell Productions. A group for new authors was formed by Nick Ligidakis to support not only their writing efforts, but also the publishing process. Meeting the other authors helped me believe writing and publishing a book was possible, and once I believed, Nick took the steps to get the book in print.

Others helped me learn the process, avoid pitfalls, and take the steps necessary to make publishing *A Trust Walk* just that. My deepest gratitude goes out to these trusted guides as well:

To the many tour professionals and amateurs who shared their experience and wisdom about the mental game and made the stories and articles come alive.

Two editors, Jim Thomas of the *Arizona Republic,* and Mark Hiland at Azcentral.com have supported my writing and provided the opportunity to write a monthly column.

Alan Korwin, a published writer himself, taught me many tricks of the writing trade while providing mentoring for my writing skills, and encouragement that I had what it takes to succeed in the world of writers.

Bill Huffman, golf writer extraordinaire, who introduced me to the world of golf writers and has guided me with wit and his own unique worldview.

My sister Patricia Turpin for her love, support and introduction to Nick and the author's group, and for being a sharp, detailed and articulate editor.

And my husband Tom Treiber, whose love surrounds me like a down comforter on a cold night, and who enthusiastically applied his graphic art talents to create the cover of the book.

Contents

Section IV: *"One of the most fascinating things about golf is how it reflects the cycle of life. No matter what you shoot, the next day you have to go back to the first tee and begin all over again and make yourself into something."*

Introduction

Folks often ask why I decided to specialize in work with golfers rather than working with athletes from all sports. The answer: I love the game of golf and the unique opportunity it provides for personal growth. Playing golf means spending four-plus hours intimately engaged with yourself. All of who you are has the time and opportunity to show up on the golf course. You meet face-to-face with the best and worst of yourself.

Golfers are constantly challenged by both inner and outer hazards to bring their best to the situation at hand. It is impossible to master golf – There's always something new to learn, and in that is the professional challenge and reward for me. Working with golfers allows me to use my skills as a psychologist to coach people to be the best they can be, and to fulfill their personal dreams and goals.

Beginning my psychology career in the 1970's meant being a part of the "sensitivity training" heyday, and the unique experiences that heralded the emergence of the "me generation." During this infamous period, "trust walks" were a common occurrence during sensitivity training sessions, and I've led or participated in many of them. Today, trust walks are an integral part of teambuilding experiences used by corporations to enhance communication among employees.

In case you have missed this adventure, let me describe a trust walk. During a trust walk you are blindfolded and led by another person through a variety of hazards. You may be led through a pine forest or across a rope bridge fifteen feet off the ground. The purpose is simple – encourage trust between two people by making the safety and well-being of one dependent on the actions of the other.

Trust is not easy to give. Many people believe it is earned, and I believe it is a gift you give or withhold after considering whether the situation at hand is congruent, or a fit, with your personal belief system. A feeling of trust emerges, and is expressed in your actions, when you interpret the situation as in line with your intentions, imagination, physical capabilities, and highest values. Sometimes the situation at hand asks that you trust someone else, as in a trust walk. Sometimes the question is whether you will trust yourself. Golf is a great venue for learning about self-trust.

Golf at its best is a trust walk with yourself. Such a walk is also known as "playing in the zone." The actions you take on the course are an accurate expression of your inner state of being.

My entire sports psychology career has been a trust walk with myself. I have believed the process of sports psychology to be meaningful, intended the facilitation of growth in others, imaged success as I defined it, acknowledged my skills, and balanced my life according to my values. This approach has served me well.

This collection of articles and stories are the result of an opportunity to write a monthly column for *The Arizona Republic,* a daily newspaper in Phoenix, and Azcentral.com, the on-line companion. In my three years as a columnist I've had the pleasure of interviewing many of the top players on the PGA and LPGA tours about the mental game of golf.

Re-reading the resulting articles I was impressed with the theme of trust that emerged: the theme of discovering what it takes to trust yourself on the golf course. Each article illuminates at least one element of the trust equation. Added together, you get the full picture of how to create inner trust, and how to consistently express it on the golf course.

The goal is to experience each round of golf as a simple trust walk with yourself amidst nature's beauty. Be mindful that when you approach golf in this way you will experience greater pleasure and lower scores. So, come along, walk with me through these pages and trust you will discover meaning within them.

<u>Section I</u>

Golf is a spiritual game.
It's like Zen.
You have to let your mind take over.
- Amy Alcott

The Lucky Ones

I am one of the lucky ones.

My luck begins with writing a column for the sports page of the *Arizona Republic*, and continues with being afforded the opportunity to meet and interview many of the top golfers on tour.

My luck reached a zenith in 1999 when, in my capacity as a columnist, I was able to walk right up to one of my all-time favorite players and ask him if he would mind spending the next half-hour or so answering my questions about the mental game of golf.

He said he'd be glad to. And so it was that I had my first of three interviews with William Payne Stewart.

Psychologists are by nature interested in human growth and development, and stories of how people overcome difficulties and create a meaningful, successful life for themselves. Because of this I had followed Payne's career with interest. I was intrigued by his individualism and the stories of how, with guts and determination, he was coming back from a career slump.

Payne always cut a dashing figure on the course, instantly recognizable in his knickers and tam-o'-shanter cap, usually flashing his engaging grin or showing his steely resolve as he marched up a fairway, or strode purposely about a green.

He was no less dashing up close. He was warm, friendly, open and engaging. He spoke thoughtfully about his personal growth of the past several years and of the new ways he had learned to help himself be more the man he wanted to be on and off the golf course.

Payne described his journey back from that time in his career when he was number 123 on the money list, in jeopardy of losing his tour card, and considering whether or not to give up golf. It was an inner journey, a journey of increased self-awareness, of making new, healthier choices, and of recapturing faith in a dream: the dream of the man God had meant him to be.

Payne used his career slump to learn, to be self-reflective and to answer anew three questions of life; *Who am I? Where am I going?* and, *Who's coming with me?* From this time of reflection he emerged with a renewed commitment and belief in himself and his goals: "I realize my time is coming, I really believe that. I'm seeing a lot of positive things out there. It's a matter of one of these weeks I'm going to click and they're gonna be watching me."

Stewart rededicated himself to his game and to his family, setting his priorities: "I'm not going to blink and miss my family growing up. When I'm out on the golf course I'm going to prepare myself to be the best I can, and when I'm home I'm going to be a father."

Professional golfer Scott Hoch saw Payne's priorities as being "in the right order," saying, "His priorities were right: God first, family second, golf third."

Payne's priorities and yours may not be exactly the same, however, deciding on a place for golf in your life that moves you toward your goals rather than away from them, is an important mental aspect of success in the game. It is an essential element of being mentally tough. Based on priorities, mentally tough people actively choose where to put their attention, knowing that where they put their attention they will make gains, in their golf game or in life.

Payne Stewart's words are the words of a mentally tough player: "If you think well enough, and realize that you don't have your 'A' game that day then you do the best with what you have. This is a learned deal – getting something positive from the bad situations. It takes a lot of mental toughness to be able to do that. If you let a pressure situation change your routine then you don't have control."

Payne got something positive from his mid-career struggles. Family, friends, fellow competitors, commentators and sports writers all spoke of the change in Stewart, and so did he when following his dramatic win at the 1999 U.S. Open he commented, "I'm so much more at peace with myself than I've ever been in my life. Where I was last year and where I am now is leaps and bounds. I'm a lot older and I'm a lot wiser. I'm more mature."

We're all the lucky ones.

We're lucky to have been able to watch Payne Stewart, the classy golfer, for all these years. We're lucky to have the opportunity to learn from his legacy: his life, his style, his answers.

Just before the U.S. Open, Stewart remarked, "I said to myself, 'Just go out there and be Payne Stewart,' and it was good enough." After the Open he said, "I don't have to change anything because now I know that I'm there. All I have to do from here on out is just believe in myself."

He was one of the lucky ones. He found himself.

And he is sorely missed.

A TRUST WALK

Mindful Golf

Ask any group of golfers the question, "How important is the mind in the game of golf?" or "What percentage of the game is mental?" and you'll hear:

"80%"

"75%"

"60%"

"It depends on your level of skill. For the pros it's about 90%, but for amateurs it's only about 30-40%."

Hale Irwin is quoted as saying, "Golf is 80% mental," and Arnold Palmer, while not giving a percentage, said, "Golf is a game of inches, and the most important are the six between your ears."

What does a sports psychologist, who gives lessons to golfers to help them with the mental game, say about this?

I say: "Golf is 100% physical AND 100% mental."

Current body/mind research clearly shows that the body and the mind are totally integrated and interactive. What happens in the body has an immediate effect on the mind, and what happens in the mind creates an immediate response in the body.

Every thought you have creates a neurochemical response in your brain and body, and every movement, even the tiniest finger movement, releases different neurotransmitters in the brain.

Some thoughts and body movements take you closer to your goals and some take you further away, but every thought and every movement takes you somewhere. The question is whether you are taking yourself where you want to go. Are you using your ability to choose, or are you just going along with old habits of thought and action?

Professional golfers are much better than amateurs at choosing thoughts and actions that give them the results they want.

Darren Clarke's win over Tiger Woods at La Costa during the Anderson Consulting World Match Play was a perfect example. Darren Clarke was 100% that day, and it was impressive to watch him succeed by remaining true to his unique style, both in his swing and in his mental approach to the game.

PGA teaching professional Butch Harmon was on hand at La Costa, coaching both Clarke and Woods on their swing mechanics, and it was interesting to note the differences in their swings, even under the tutorage of the same coach.

Woods exhibits smooth, flowing power, while Clarke's swing is more like a hard right jab! Both swings work, and Harmon's job is to maximize the result of each man's swing while honoring and supporting his uniqueness.

Honor what works for you, and you encourage your body/mind to work well and to experience a sense of trust, flow, or being "in sync."

Darren Clarke was in sync.

Tiger Woods was out of sync.

I bet that most of you have taken some swing lessons, had a friend "coach" you, read golf magazines or watched golf on TV. You want to choose how to swing your golf club to make the best shots possible, and to be able to evaluate and correct things when you get out of sync.

But I've asked several hundred golfers another question: "How many of you have EVER gone to the practice tee or out on the golf course with the intention to practice your mental skills?"

Only three people out of hundreds raised their hands.

Not many practice "mindful golf."

When asked, "Why don't you practice mental skills?" the reply is usually something like, "I don't know what to practice, or how to practice what I know."

Perhaps a lesson might help.

There are three basic mental skills that I help my golfers remember and use to improve their game and make it more fun: self-awareness, choice, and imagination. Each skill has many facets and individual permutations, and the lessons are individualized to fit the needs of each golfer. That is the art of being a Head Coach®.

But even without taking lessons from a mental skills coach you can begin to know what to practice, and practice what you know, by following these guidelines:

1. Go out and play one round of golf with the purpose of noticing your self-talk. Simply notice what you say to yourself in your mind and then notice the results of that communication on your golf game. _Do not try to change anything, just notice._

2. During another game notice what your playing partners say to themselves and to you, and its effect on their golf game. Do you notice any correlation between what they say and how they play? What about a correlation between their words and their level of pleasure, or your pleasure being with them? What about effects on _your_ game?

3. For one round of golf decide that you will intentionally hold your target in your imagination for each and every shot or putt. By "holding it in your imagination" I mean that as you stand over your shot you simply and gently "remember" where you want the ball to

go. Remembering in this way might mean you have a *picture* of the target in your mind, or you might have a *sense* of the target in your mind, or you might hear the *sound* the clubface will make to propel the ball to the target in your mind. There is no right or wrong or good or bad way to "remember," there is only the way that works best for you.

Tiger Woods credits his father, and a sports psychologist, Jay Brunza, with helping him develop the mental skills of a winner, and I don't know if Darren Clarke works with a sports doc or not, but most of the pros do.

What I can guarantee is that both of them have developed great skill in being aware of what works for them, actively choosing what's in their best interest, and intentionally using their imagination to actively rehearse desired outcomes as a way to listen to their intuition.

By doing so they increase the amount of the time they are in sync on the golf course. So can you.

Shrink Your Golf Score

If you're a serious golfer you've probably spent time and money on a teaching pro, club fitting, and practicing to groove a trusted swing. However, you probably have not purposely and skillfully learned or practiced the mental skills that would lower your scores and increase your pleasure on the course.

If you follow the golf pros on TV (and what avid golfer doesn't?), then you've heard the talk about players who work with a sports psychologist. Sometimes they give their "head coach," "sports doc," or "shrink," some credit for their improved play or even for a tournament victory.

Professional and amateur golfers seek out a sports psychologist for two reasons: first, to help them get unstuck when things are not going well in their game, and second, to help them get the "winner's edge" when things are going very well indeed.

An important part of the coaching job is to help players identify how their mind prevents them from playing at their best. A mental coach can help a player determine what's happening when they're stuck, and provide insight and support in creating a plan to get back on track.

What surprises most players is the number of professional and amateur golfers who seek mental skills training when their game is as good as it's ever been. These players are seeking performance enhancement. They want a winner's edge to put them in position to grab the brass ring – whatever that may mean for them.

John (not his real name) plays at various courses around the valley, and his goal is to be recognized as one of the top amateurs in Phoenix. He read one of my articles and decided to give me a call. He was a 10 handicap who wanted to get to a three or less in 12 months. His long-range goal was to qualify as an amateur on the Goldwater Cup team.

He has been working with the same swing coach for several years and believes in his swing – trusting it most of the time. He said his problem was an inability to stay focused over each shot for a full round of golf. Using self-awareness exercises and education about how the body responds to the mind (and vice versa) John was able to increase his trust in his mind, and perform better on the course. He's currently playing to a six handicap and plans to continue to see me every other month to refresh his commitment to use his mind while playing golf. My money is on him for reaching his goal and playing in the Goldwater Cup next year.

Max (also not his real name) was referred to me by his teaching pro; the pro felt Max had taken his physical game as far as he could. He told Max that the next step was to use his mind as effectively as he could swing his clubs. Max told me his anger got in the way on the golf course. As a kid he was a club thrower, now he was a club "thumper," thumping his club on the ground if he didn't like his shot. While thumping, he would also say a few choice words and then proceed to double-bogey the next hole.

Max and I did a lot of talking about anger and its roots. He was surprised to learn that anger is a second feeling, and the first feeling is fear. This was not easy for a big, burly man (6'2," 255 lbs.), to accept. In fact, he got angry! It was his anger at that moment that helped him realize that fear was behind his angry reaction. He was afraid he would look like a sissy if he admitted he was afraid. A real catch twenty-two.

Max opened himself to the possibility that fear was the culprit. Whenever he felt angry he would ask himself what fear was present. His coaching continues and he reports many fewer club thumping experiences. He's also more relaxed on the golf course, and his

10

buddies have commented that he is more fun to play with now. A final example, Jane (right, its not her real name either), plays on the second team for her country club and is losing more often than winning. She's been playing six years and carries a 24 handicap. Since team play is flighted, Jane is playing against women with similar skill levels to her own. Her teaching pro helped her realize that if she worked on her mental golf skills she would have an advantage over her competitors. She came to see me.

I met Jane at her golf club and we went out on the course. She played nine holes while I observed. I was struck by the frequency of negative, self-deprecating things she said to herself. On hole number five I asked her to stop for a quick exercise. She agreed. I asked her to close her eyes and center her attention on her body. She was to notice any physical sensations. While she was quiet, her attention centered on her body sensations, I began to say the single word "no." I used various tones and loudness: "No. No. No!" After a brief pause I shifted to repeating the word "yes," again varying my tone and loudness.

When Jane opened her eyes I asked what sensations she noticed in her body as I said "No" and "Yes." She reported (as do most people) that the word "no" created tension and tightness in her body while the word "yes" caused sensations of ease and comfort.

Next I asked her, "If your body responds to just those single words strongly enough that you can feel it, what do you imagine happens inside your body when you tell yourself you are stupid, incapable, or clumsy?

Jane had never thought of that before, but she would from that day forward.

If you are spending all your time and energy perfecting your golf swing, and ignoring your mental golf game, you may be ignoring the very thing you need to take your game to the next level. It takes both your mind and your body to play golf, and it takes practicing both to lower your golf score.

11

A TRUST WALK

The Favorite

Phil Mickelson was a favorite from start to finish during the 2000 Williams World Challenge golf tournament at Grayhawk Golf Club in Scottsdale, Arizona.

At the start he was a favorite, not just because he is a well-liked local pro, but also because the tournament was being played on his home course and everyone thought that might give him an edge.

He was a favorite at the finish because he made what may be the shot of the century: after watching Mark O'Meara four-putt on the hail-covered 18th green, Mickelson holed a 25-foot putt by choosing to use his L-wedge to chip it into the cup.

However, in between the start and the finish things did not go so well for the popular Scottsdale pro. It was a continuation of what he called a "disappointing golf year." He said, "It was the first year that I went without a win."

His response to the disappointment?

"I spent a lot of time working on my game last year, and the particular areas or individual areas of my game improved dramatically. I drove the ball much more accurately than I have. I've increased distance. My sand game is improved. Putting improved. But yet I didn't win. Statistically, as an all-around player, I felt like I became much better, but I didn't win," said Mickelson.

What's left? What's next?

The next step was clear in his mind as he said, "I need to improve my mental outlook. I need more mental toughness. That's the area where I really need to improve. Whether it's on the green or one or two erratic drives, I need to be mentally tough on every shot. And that's where last year I failed. And that's why I didn't win."

The term "mental toughness," gets tossed around a lot and means different things to different people. When asked what it meant to him, Mickelson said it meant he was going to work on "better focus and being better prepared when I need it."

Davis Love III and Hal Sutton were also competing at the Williams World Challenge. These tour veterans also had some thoughts about mental toughness and the importance it plays in their game:

"I'm set in my ways," said Love, "I have a routine for my full swing, my short shots, putting, that I go through every time. Doing the same thing over and over and over. That is my safety net. But it's what you're thinking and where your head's at. I just try to get into my target."

"I want to be focused on playing the game," continued Love, "rather than being focused on the mechanics of my swing. If you're thinking about your swing, you're gonna get off-and-on results. You'll be trying to fix things rather than playing golf. If you're focused on your target, you can do a pretty good job."

Love believes it's important to "get into the process rather than the results." He added, "If you're thinking about the process you won't be thinking about the past or the future. If you start thinking about how tough the next hole is, or what happens if I hit it in the lake, or the only way I'm going to chip this ball close is if I chip it in, or things like that, you're not into your target."

And if you find yourself into results rather than process? "Any thought that's not right is a trigger," said Love, "Let everything be a reminder to get you back where you want to go."

Hal Sutton said he likes to "try to stay on an even keel, not expecting too much or too little." He continued, "I stay one shot at a time, not getting ahead of myself... if you get outside the present you're aware of all the wrong things." And not staying in the present can be disastrous said Sutton, "If you're just one hole too late in being present, sometimes that's the difference between finishing 2nd, 3rd 5th, or however. The quicker you notice the better you finish."

It's a challenge to notice when you've left the present. Sutton's recommendation? He said, "We try hard all the time to stay focused on what we're doing and remember all the things we know it takes to play well, but invariably we forget and have to be reminded by somebody. I think the key is realizing that you can't do it all by yourself. You have to listen to the people around you, and the people can't be afraid to say what they're feeling either. They have to be honest and tell you what they're thinking, and you have to be open enough to listen to what they're saying."

Sutton's final word on the matter: "Ninety percent of the time you don't learn anything new, you just get reminded of things you used to know."

Words of a wise coach.

Perhaps Phil Mickelson's miracle shot on the 18th green can remind him of what he knows and maybe has forgotten about mental toughness.

It takes the mental toughness of a major champion to stand on the green in a hailstorm, watch your playing partner four-putt, and be present enough to enjoy the moment just as it is, keep your attention on the target, trust yourself to create the unique shot you want, and make it!

That's mental toughness in a nutshell – or maybe in a hailstorm.

A TRUST WALK

<u>Section II</u>

There can be no happiness
if the things we believe in are
different from the things we do
- *Freya Stark*

A TRUST WALK

Inner Adventures

I have something in common with researchers at the University of Chicago; I get excited about examining and understanding the brains of golfers. The researchers are hoping to use the knowledge gained from research with golfers to rehabilitate victims of stroke and other neurological disorders.

The researchers and I also share an interest (in my case it's a fascination) with the power of imagery. They are using a relatively new technology called functional magnetic resonance imaging (FMRI) to study the ability of golfers to visualize and complete a difficult task. The FMRI lets them see what's going on in the brain of the player. I like to think it lets them record the golfers' *inner adventures*. The images show the researchers which parts of the brain are functioning when a task is being performed, even if the task is only happening in the person's imagination.

Many coaches have long believed that practicing an activity in your imagination produces a practice effect which improves performance. The research being done in Chicago, along with other studies currently in progress, is a step toward scientific confirmation of that belief.

There is much to be learned from an understanding and application of imagery to the sport of golf.

Imagery is defined as any sensory thought form; this means that visualization is only one type of imagery. In fact, many confused people believe they cannot use imagery if they are unable to see pictures in their minds' eye.

In fact, you use your imagination every day, all day. You visualize something; you sense something; you get a feeling; you hear an intuitive knowing inside yourself. These are all ways of imagining!

There are four distinct ways you can use your imagination on the golf course:

1. **Passive imagination** *(intuition)*: Have you ever walked up to a putt and known even before you stroked the ball, that it was going to fall into the hole? That's an example of passive imagery – it is your intuition telling you conciously what it knows at an unconscious level. Listen to those gut feelings on the course, whether it's which club to choose or what target to pick for your next shot.

2. **Active imagination** *(performance rehearsal and imaginary practice)*: Many golfers find it improves their score if they imagine each shot prior to actually swinging the club or making a stroke with their putter. Some players will *see* the ball in flight and landing at the choosen target; others may *hear* the clubface striking the ball with the sound associated with a specific type of shot. Another player may simply have a *sense* of the shot they wish to perform, while their partner is busy *feeling* the shot they want to make, or *watching* themselves as if they were on camera.

The practice tee is a great place to exercise your imagination. Spend at least half of your practice time playing a round of golf in your imagination. Imagine a specific hole, go through your pre-shot process, select a club, choose a target, and make the shot. Watch the ball fly and imagine where it comes to rest on the fairway. In your imagination, walk up to the ball, determine the club for your second shot, create a unique lie, choose a target, and make your second shot. Keep playing in your mind until you've made it to the green.

Vary the imaginary holes you play and the shots you are required to make.

Remember, no one way of imagining is better than another. What is most important is to recognize your personal and natural style of imagining and apply that process to your golf game.

3. **Receptive imagery** *(purposely inviting and listening to the wisdom within)*: This process is much like when you have a problem on your mind and suddenly something provides you with an answer. Perhaps you find the answer in a book you are reading on a topic unrelated to the problem, or you hold a problem in mind prior to going to bed and awaken the next morning to discover the answer fully formed in your mind. These are examples of receptive imagery at work.

The next time you are playing golf and find yourself unsure, or in conflict about a decision, try this exercise: walk a few feet away from your playing partners, turn your awareness inside and invite a connection with the wisdom that resides there. Invite an image to come to mind that represents the problem and has information about solutions. Accept whatever image comes; don't try to make one appear, just be curious and open to whatever happens. Know that the image can come in any sensory form. A picture of something could appear, or you might have a sense of something being present. Just accept what comes.

Listen for whatever notions, ideas or suggestions are provided and see if they are helpful to the situation at hand. Maintain an attitude of open curiosity and trust, and you will be surprised at what you discover.

4. **Interactive imagery** *(inner dialogue)*: We talk to ourselves constantly during the day. Those dialogues are sometimes fully conscious and sometimes outside of our direct awareness.

Worry is the most common form of interactive imagery. We often experience worry as a technicolor motion picture with surround-sound projected in the mind. We create characters, give them crafted dialogue and direct the action, usually leading to the most feared result. And your body reacts as if what you are imaging is actually happening: sweaty palms, clamped jaw, gritted teeth, flushed skin

21

and racing heart.

This also happens on the golf course, and you can learn to purposely and skillfully create an inner dialogue that is helpful rather than one that causes havoc.

You might consider creating an "inner coach," by inviting an image that is wise and skilled in the game of golf to emerge from your unconscious. Your inner coach is always available to be by your side. You can ask questions, listen to answers, and discuss whatever golf problem you are facing. Working with your coach, produce the movie you want: the movie with the snappy, witty dialogue and inevitable happy ending.

Inner Coaching

"Earl of Scotland," was his name, and my client, Bob, met him on a Tuesday morning as he sat in my golf-cart office beside the practice tee. Earl had some things in common with literary golf favorites such as Shivas Irons of _Golf in the Kingdom,_ and Baggar Vance from _The Legend of Baggar Vance._ Yet Earl was clearly unique. Earl came from Bob's intuitive imagination and represented his personal image of an "inner coach." Over the next several months Earl became Bob's trusted inner companion on the links.

How did Bob meet and get to know Earl? Through training in a mental skills process known as **_Interactive Guided Imagery_**sm. There are a variety of skills intended to help people achieve more success in sports and life, and _Interactive Imagery_sm is one of the finest available. Developed by Martin Rossman, M.D., and David Bresler, Ph.D., _Interactive Imagery_sm is the modality of choice for over 500 practitioners certified by the _Academy for Guided Imagery_™. Those practitioners teach people to access and use their inner resources to create health and well-being.

The use of inner images is hardly a new concept. Since the 13th century, or even earlier, Buddhists have used imagery as a spiritual way to be in touch with the highest and best of who they are and their inner wisdom.

Only in more recent history has imagery been actively accepted and used in our Western culture. The popularity of the process has been spearheaded by health-care providers, and has quickly been adopted by other professionals in corporate training and sports psychology.

Bob was in the early stages of an imagery experience when he met Earl. I gave Bob a few relaxation suggestions, invited him to get comfortable, and asked him to be quiet inside. Bob then imagined a favorite golf hole, and invited an image of a wise and skilled coach to join him on the tee box.

Earl showed up!

Bob began to "talk" with Earl and liked him right away. This kind of dialogue is like the ones you have in your mind when you are problem-solving or worrying about something: you imagine talking to someone about the problem or the source of worry. You use your imagination in similar ways every day of your life. Imaging and talking with a golf coach is really nothing new, it's just that you usually don't imagine as purposely or skillfully as what I'm describing.

Think for a minute of all the times you've imagined an action or dialogue, or you've had daydreams or nightdreams that contained important information. And certainly you have had your share of experience with the two most popular forms of imagery: worry and fantasy.

*Interactive Imagery*sm uses the same natural mental process in a skillful and positive manner to create the results you want, or to gain information about a problem you hold in mind.

Over the next couple of months Bob shared many stories with me about Earl. He was impressed with their relationship and the trust that had developed between them. He told me of one experience that took place on a chilly overcast day during the second round of a 3-day amateur tournament:

Bob, three shots off the lead, was on the 7th tee, a short par three, when he pushed his shot into the greenside bunker.

Bob had not yet talked to Earl during this round although he sensed his presence with him. But now, noticing the increased inner anxiety, he wanted some help. Earl was "Johnny-on-the-spot."

Bob had learned to take a breath, let a question come to mind, and then wait for an answer from Earl. Bob's question on this hole was, "How can I handle this anxiety I'm feeling?"

Earl pointed out that Bob was remembering the last tournament when he blew a bunker shot and missed a 2nd place finish.

Earl suggested that Bob choose to remember a bunker shot he had played well; image it, pick his target (the hole) and make his shot. Bob did. The ball flew true and landed inches from the pin. An easy par.

Bob went on to finish 2nd and was excited that he had learned one more way to deal with anxiety on the course.

Bob regularly practiced his mental skills, and one way he practiced was playing golf with Earl in his imagination. His second story was about one of those times:

Bob and Earl were discussing Bob's golf goals. Earl helped Bob discover that he had a tendency to set goals for what he **should do** *instead of what he* **wanted to do.**

Earl encouraged Bob to set goals for what he **wanted,** *and when he began to do so Bob noticed that he was more smooth and trusting with his swing. His handicap also dropped from a 20 to a 15 in six months time.*

Bob learned to use Interactive Imagery⁣sm in two ways: actively, as when he rehearsed playing in his best form, and receptively, as when images like Earl were invited to bring helpful information and problem-solve.

You too have an **inner coach** ready and willing to be your mental skills guide on and off the golf course. *Just imagine, your own personal inner coach,* what a great addition to your game that would be!

A TRUST WALK

Just Imagine ... "Armchair Practice"

Listen to a group of amateur golfers and you'll almost always hear them say, "I never have enough time to practice and play as much as I want to."

Does that sound like you?

Do you wish you could find more time to polish your game?

That's exactly what Tom said when he came to see me a few weeks before a big tournament.

He's the CEO of a thriving company, a competitive man who lives by the motto, "If I'm going to do it, I'm going to do it right!"

One of Tom's frustrations is not enough time for practice. "It's hard to get away right now; we're in the middle of a big sales promotion, and I have to be at the office even more than usual. How am I going to get ready for our club championship?" Tom continued, "What I need is a way to practice without leaving home or the office: something I can do when I have just a few minutes to spare."

So I introduced him to "Armchair Practice," which is *daydreaming with a purpose.* It's using your imagination to creatively practice your skills.

Using imagery to rehearse a performance is certainly not new, nor is it my invention. It is a process often used by elite athletes in many sports, most notably by Olympians. It is well researched and documented that practicing your sport performance while relaxed, and using all of your senses, has a dramatic practice effect.

27

The recent winter Olympics offered many opportunities to observe athletes who were obviously mentally rehearsing. Figure skaters, bobsledders, downhill ski racers, snowboarders and cross-country ski racers were shown with their eyes closed, bodies gently moving, as they imagined themselves moving through their performance.

With Tom, I sent him out to play a practice round on the tournament course, and had him take several photographs of each hole: one from the tee box, another of the fairway, and one of the green.

He made the photos into a scrapbook, with each of the eighteen holes on a single 8-1/2x11 sheet of paper. The pages were stapled together and he could flip through them just like a book.

In the weeks prior to the tournament, Tom imagined his golf performance at least once a day by looking at the pictures of each of the individual golf holes.

Each practice session began with Tom settling into a comfortable chair, relaxing, doing a simple but effective relaxation process he learned (one that's uniquely his own), and deciding which hole(s) he wants to play. Staying relaxed, he briefly opens his eyes to look at the pictures of the hole he's going to play, and he imagines himself moving onto the tee box.

Once on the tee box, he experiences his pre-shot routine in detail, not just through *visualization*, or what he "sees" in his mind's eye, but also using all of his other senses.

His awareness includes his muscles firing, tightening and releasing, the feel of his feet on the ground, and perhaps a sense of the ground being either soft or hard. Aromas in the air, like freshly mowed grass, become apparent to him, along with the slight breeze that ruffles his hair.

He hears spectators as they stand whispering behind the tee, the announcer calling his name, and even an airplane above his head.

Some of you may think that if you do not "see pictures in your mind" that you are unable to do imagery. In fact, it is not uncommon for people who do not have pictures in their mind to learn to use imagery quite effectively. Visualization is only one way in which imagery occurs. Many people using *imagery* have a "sense of something being present" but do not have a *picture* of something being present. It does not matter how your imagery comes to you. There is no right, wrong, better or best way to image.

Tom "experiences" his stance, the "just right" grip pressure and the perfect aim. He sees or senses his take-away and backswing, the slight pause at the top, the energy shift and momentum of the downswing, and the stretch and sense of total balance during follow-thru.

He "hears" the whoosh of the club head and solid impact as clubface meets ball, and the swish as the ball flies into the air. He "feels" himself standing poised and "watching" the flight of the ball and the perfect landing as it hits and rolls, stopping within inches of the target.

He plays the entire hole, "sensing" himself walking down the fairway, putting, and finally hearing that most wonderful of sounds: the rattle of the ball as it falls in the cup!

Later, after the tournament, Tom recalled feeling confident as the announcer spoke his name and he stepped onto the first tee. He described the feeling like this: "I'd been there before, and it went well!"

During the tournament he felt focused, with just enough adrenaline flow to give him a sense of the "winners edge." He played well each of the three days of the tournament as the positive sense of deja vu remained vibrant within him.

Shooting a 70, 78, and 72 respectively, and placing second overall, he's proud of his accomplishment. He *imagines* that next year he will be the champion!

Now that he has discovered a time-saving way to practice he will get in more practice time and his confidence and consistency will

29

go up while his handicap goes down.

Just imagine, he has a very real chance of making that championship **a reality**! Especially if he continues to daydream with a purpose and use his **armchair practice** to enhance his performance!

Just Imagine ... You're Energized!!

Just imagine, it's Thursday morning, your golf day, and before work you load your clubs into the trunk of the car anticipating an early afternoon tee time. Setting off to work you feel energized with the anticipation of being on the links later in the day.

You spend four hours caught up in the typical frenzy of work; your cranky boss is tossing barbs around the office, and so many land on you that you feel like someone put a bull's-eye on your shirt.

By noon, when you're ready to leave for the course, it's like someone removed your battery. You have to drag yourself to the car. Harried, frazzled, and stressed are understatements for the tight muscles and racing thoughts in your head: "Should I go? There's so much I need to do at work. Maybe this isn't a good time to go play golf. Will my boss be angry? I'll never be able to keep my mind on the game."

By the time you're in the car you feel so drained that it's hard to imagine hitting a golf ball at all, much less hitting it where you want it!

Time for lunch? No way. You'll get the bag boys to grab a sandwich for you and put it in your cart to eat on the course.

Warm up? Again, no way. It's going to be a "trunk-to-tee" golf day.

Typically, this scenario would mean disaster on the course. Your inner chaos would be expressed in wild and erratic golf shots–the kind that can make even the most mild-mannered person mutter obscenities and quit golf every other week.

But today is not your typical day. Oh sure, the stage is the same, but today you have a different script. It goes like this:

You leave work and slide behind the steering wheel of your car. The first thing you notice is a sticky note you placed in the center of your steering wheel after you parked at the office this morning. The note is a reminder of your commitment to make new choices today. You smile to yourself remembering.

You speak the first line of your new script, saying to yourself: "I *want* to play golf today, and my intention is to be energized and fully present to the experience, which begins NOW!"

On the way to the course you use each stop light as an opportunity to do a body scan, focusing your attention, and *intention,* on relaxing the tension in each part of your body.

You roll your head from side to side in a slow circular motion, letting it drop forward as you move it from one side to the other. You flex your fingers, releasing the death grip on your steering wheel, and shrug your shoulders several times. You release tension in your jaw by opening and closing your mouth. You listen to soothing music, and notice the natural beauty going past your window. You recall your favorite round of golf, and you *breathe.* You feel the air inhaled deeply into your abdominal area, and while you exhale you imagine the release of tension and removal of toxins from your body.

You arrive at the course 20 minutes before your assigned tee time. You drop off your clubs and put on your shoes. You have about 10 minutes left. Your highest priority, based on the intention written on your sticky note, is to spend the time creating a positive inner energy.

Choosing a place where you will be undisturbed (*e.g.,* sitting in your car, or on the bumper of the open trunk, in a golf cart, or a corner of the locker-room), you close your eyes and invite your body to relax more and more with each breath you take.

Now you recall a time in your life when you experienced the inner positive energy that you desire for today's round of golf. You notice where you are and what you are doing. You notice the specific qualities that are present in the energy. You may feel clear-headed, focused, tingly with anticipation, warm, confident, or wise.

There are no right, wrong, better, or best qualities to have – there are only those qualities which are present in *your* imagination. You accept the qualities that come, as long as they represent your desired state of positive energy. If they don't, you simply recall a different experience, one which does bring forth the qualities you want.

Now you imagine "stepping into yourself" in the remembered experience, and you invite an awareness of the positive energy flowing through your body. You notice and experience each of the qualities in turn, thanking them for being present.

Remaining quiet, you imagine your newly energized self on the first tee of today's golf course. You image yourself in great detail, calling upon all of your senses to make the experience as real as possible. You notice the feel of the grass under your feet, the warm sun on your back, the gentle breeze ruffling your hair. You see the fairway, and pick a target. You feel the texture of the grip in your hand, and the weight of the club as you lift it from the bag.

You tee off and watch the flight of the ball as it soars in the air, lands and rolls right to your target.

You open your eyes, (if you had them closed) and head for the first tee. As you stand on the tee, you simply notice that you have successfully recharged your batteries and re-energized yourself, just as you imagined and intended!

What could have been a disastrous day of golf has been saved by your attention and invention. You have made new choices. You have changed your energy and your day by using your imagination. Never let a lousy day at the office ruin a great day of golf, and never let one lousy shot ruin your whole round. You now know you can choose the focus of your energy.

Clear the Mechanism

"Clear the mechanism," says Billy Chapel, a professional baseball player played by Kevin Costner in his movie, *For Love of the Game*. Costner's character is a professional pitcher with 19 years on the mound; he is looking at what might be his last major league ball-game.

The setting of the movie hits close to home for Arizona baseball fans: the action takes place during a fictional final game of a divisional championship playoff series between the New York Yankees and Costner's team, the Detroit Tigers.

The Tigers meet the Yankees at Yankee Stadium, and the New York fans are portrayed as relentless, loud and obnoxious in their torment of the Tiger players, especially Chapel, who stands on the mound determined to take the game away from the home team.

Amid the deafening roar of the crowd, Chapel is shown taking a deep breath and saying to himself, "Clear the mechanism." The world around him immediately retreats, becoming blurred and eerily quiet. The viewer has the impression of a tunnel running from Chapel to home plate and the catcher. With those three simple words, Chapel has relegated everything else to the background.

The quiet, the blurred background, and the clarity of focus are the result of the simple intention to shift his awareness, his attention, to the space between himself, the batter and the catcher. Chapel is using what golfers call a "swing key" to focus his attention where he wants it, thus creating a desired foreground and moving everything else into the background of his awareness.

Please notice two very important characteristics about the process: the key itself does **not** involve the <u>mechanics</u> of pitching a ball, and no effort is made to *block out* distractions. His effort and intention are placed squarely in a process that uses a mental trigger (the words: "clear the mechanism") to alert his mind to his target.

The mental trigger is the way he reminds himself, prior to pitching, to place his attention where he wants it to be. It's a form of quick induction for self-hypnosis. Hypnosis, a natural skill we all possess, is simply a change in your state of consciousness and focus.

Everyone can, and does, enter trance states on a daily basis, just not on purpose. I'm sure you can recall experiences like: being deeply engrossed in the simple pleasure of watching clouds meander across the sky; skipping dinner because you were so involved in a book that you were transported to another place and time; arriving home with the sudden realization that you can't remember how you got there (and you're clean and sober). In these situations, and countless others you can probably describe, you were in a trance state.

Being "in the zone" is a trance experience you hear described by athletes, including golfers. They talk about a performance seeming effortless and easy, almost like they aren't even there. They may report being enveloped in a cocoon of concentration where time is distorted and things of importance are vividly clear.

In golf, the "trance" may last only from the beginning of your pre-shot routine to the moment the clubhead strikes the ball, or it may extend over several holes of play. Rarely do you hear a golfer say they played an entire round "in the zone."

I bet that Justin Leonard entered the zone during the 1999 Ryder Cup, certainly for the winning putt on number 17, but likely at a time prior to that. And maybe it was his friend, Davis Love III, saying encouraging words that became his "swing key," and provided the trigger to shift his awareness and consciousness to a vividly clear target.

Have you had the experience of putting so well that the hole actually seems larger than at other times, and of *knowing* a given putt will fall even before you stroke the ball? You've been in trance.

You can also put yourself into a negative trance state, and I'm sure you've played with people who do this. They're the ones who talk to themselves constantly, silently and out loud, saying how bad they are, how rotten their swing is, how the wheels have come off, and the car is up on jacks. They narrow their focus, put their attention in one direction, and they, too, are in trance.

Which trance experience do you want?

I wonder if Kevin Costner, who plays in celebrity pro-ams across the country, learned from his baseball role how to use a solid pre-shot process, a non-mechanical swing key, and positive self-talk to put himself in the best frame of mind for the golf course. Listen carefully the next time you watch him play and see if you can catch the whispered, "Clear the mechanism," just before he lets the big dog eat.

A TRUST WALK

Body Talk

You and I know that positive self-talk plays an important role in achieving success on the golf course. You've heard the sayings a million times: "You are what you think you are," "As you think so shall you be," "Think and grow rich (successful)," and "If you think you can, or you think you can't, you're right either way!"

In other words, our bodies (behavior) are affected by what we believe and say in our minds. Research in the field of mind/body health leaves little doubt as to the accuracy of this notion. But did you know that it also works the other way around?

THE MIND IS AFFECTED BY WHAT HAPPENS IN THE BODY.

The first frame of one of my favorite Peanuts cartoons shows Charlie Brown, and his body language shouts to the world that he's depressed. While his sister Sally looks on, Charlie Brown stands with his shoulders slumped and his head down, and says to her that this is the way to stand when you're depressed.

In the next frame, he explains that when you're depressed it makes a lot of difference how you stand. As he tells Sally, "The absolute worst thing you can do is stand straight and hold your head high." Why? As Charlie Brown says, "If you stand straight and hold your head up high, you'll start to feel better!"

He can't behave that way and still feel depressed!

In the final frame, he tells Sally that if you're going to get any joy out of being depressed, you've got to stand like you're depressed.

39

Have you noticed golfers who look totally dejected after a missed shot or two? Maybe you've experienced it yourself? You walk away from a shot with your head down, shoulders slumped, slamming clubs in the ground with a frown on your face. Your body is sending a negative message to your mind. Perhaps the message is one of giving up, or not trusting yourself, and that creates the possibility that your game will get worse.

Watching other golfers, even the pros, you can often tell from their body expressions exactly when they are "out of the match." It might be following a double or triple bogey, or perhaps the third bogey in a row, or maybe it was an eight on a blowup hole. Regardless, the body language tells the story of the mortal wound. You've probably even commented on it to your buddies, "He looks out of it now!" And he probably is.

Our body communicates using the language of "sensation." A sensation is a chemically-based stimulation that lets you know when your body wants or needs something, like food, water, or sleep. The body clearly signals when something is wrong, using pain or discomfort to get your attention. When you are afraid, no matter the source of the fear, your body automatically responds with the fight or flight syndrome. Your heart rate increases, adrenaline is released, and you prepare to either fight or run.

Any physical sensation or symptom that you experience is a message from your body attempting to provide you information and encouragement. At times the symptoms insist you pay attention and do something to restore balance and health.

By now you might be asking, "Which comes first, the self-talk or the body language?" Is the body language "negative" because of your thoughts about a certain shot, or did you come to the course carrying a negative "body attitude" that has affected your shot-making? The body/mind is integrated and interactive, and therefore it is often impossible to tell which came first. The important thing to remember is that in either case you can choose behavior which is more likely to create the result you want. One way to do that is to follow the old adage that says "Fake it till you make it."

Try the following exercise the next time you are headed to the course directly from a difficult time at home or the office:

First, notice how your body is behaving. Are your movements quick, jerky, or angry? Is the tone of your voice harsh, your speech quick? Are your muscles tight and tense? Do you have a death grip on the steering wheel? Is your pulse rate higher than normal? Notice your shoulders. Are they bunched up and tense? Do you have a frown on your face?

Notice the sensations in your body and remind yourself that these body expressions are creating messages to your mind. If you behave a certain way then your beliefs and your feelings will begin to align themselves with that behavior. Now ask yourself the important question: "Is that what I want to have happen right now?" Answer that question, and choose body expressions that will send the message you want.

Take some deep breaths. Invite your body to become calm and comfortable. Smile. Hold the steering wheel with just enough pressure to get the job done. Count to ten slowly. Put on some soothing music. Slow down by five miles per hour. Let someone in front of you. Focus on your shoulder muscles and invite them to soften and smooth. At stop lights, look outside and notice the beauty around you. Relax your jaw. Wiggle your toes. Tell yourself a joke or a story that makes you laugh.

You can decide to have your body speak a different language: the language of confidence, the language of well-being. What do you want your body telling your mind on the golf course? It's up to you. When you want to feel more positive on the golf course, choose to have your body speak with a language of confidence and well-being. Keep your head up, shoulders squared, and a determined, confident eye on your next target.

Remember, "If you believe you can or you believe you can't, you're right either way," AND, if you *act as if you can or act as if you can't,* again you are right either way!

A TRUST WALK

See What You Believe

I live on a golf course. One day I heard the clank, clatter, and crash of a golf ball ricocheting off my house; I looked out just in time to see it roll off the roof and drop, kerplunk, into the deep end of the swimming pool.

Getting balls out of the pool is a regular occurrence, and requires a simple trip to get the skimmer and a fishing expedition for the ball. As I started into the other room to get my shoes, I saw the golfer who owned the drowned ball drive up to the fence that separates our yard from the course.

I watched as he looked around the yard and noticed his ball in the deep end of the pool. Before I could get the door open, or say a word to him about rescuing his poor, soaked ball, he hefted his golf club, held it horizontally in both hands, and brought it down over his knee, breaking the shaft cleanly in half.

I thought about taking him my business card, but decided it wasn't a safe moment to suggest mental skills coaching to this angry, red-faced man who held half of a club in each fist. He muttered to his playing partner as they drove away, and I noticed his companion wasn't saying a word either.

Golf seems unique in its ability to reduce even the most brave soul to this sad display of pitiful defeat.

What is it about golf that can capture and delight us, even as it can drive us to distraction, obsession, and anger?

Recently, a client I'll call George asked me that exact question: "How can I keep from getting so angry on the golf course? It is hurting my friendships, and I know it gets in my way during tournaments."

George didn't break clubs; he just threw them around – like into the lake!

Some of our discussion went as follows:

"George," I asked, "what do you suppose causes your anger on the golf course?" "It just happens," he answered, "I'm going along and everything seems okay then I make a stupid shot or miss a shot and my blood just starts boiling! This is such a stupid game. No matter how hard I try I can't seem to get it right! *GOLF MAKES ME SO MAD!"*

Golf *makes* him mad.

I challenged that notion. I suggested that golf, the game itself, is always perfect; it is just there, a wide open possibility. Anyone can walk out on a course and create an experience for themselves, pleasant or unpleasant.

So where does anger come from?

Anger is a naturally occurring emotion: it is a feeling that arises when you are hurt or afraid and unwilling (or unable) to directly express your hurt or fear. Anger, then, is a "second" feeling. Hurt or fear comes first, and either is usually harder to share than anger because you feel more vulnerable expressing them.

Let's look at this concept more closely.

You play golf because you desire a certain expeience on the golf course. Your intention may change at different times and for each particular round of golf you play.

Your intention may be "hit and giggle" golf – played for the social fun of it, or to be outdoors just enjoying the scenery and your playing partners. Another round may be about competition: with yourself or in a tournament. In the latter case, your intention is to win, however you define "winning." Or you might be playing "business" golf, where your focus is on networking with colleagues or entertaining a valued customer.

When you play golf, under any circumstances, you have a preferred experience that you want to happen. **The less the actual experience fits the desired experience the greater the opportunity for hurt and fear to show up, and, subsequently, anger to be present.**

Notice I said, "the opportunity for anger" shows up, not the anger itself. We do not automatically become hurt, fearful or angry when a situation doesn't fit our desire. Those feelings are the result of our interpretation of a given situation.

> *"People are disturbed not by events but*
> *by their interpretations of these events."*
> *- Epictetus*

When you snap-hook a ball, dump one in the water, hit it out of bounds, miss a three-foot putt, take a ten on a par four, or anything else that isn't part of your desired experience, you get to **choose** what you think about that situation. **You will experience what you believe to be true.**

What you think and believe about what has happened is what causes feelings. Feelings, in turn, cause you to behave in a certain way.

Beliefs create feelings and feelings create behaviors.

Some of the beliefs that create feelings of hurt, fear and, secondarily, anger in golfers are the following:

- *I really have to impress this guy or gal.*

- *I've practiced hard and that old snap-hook shouldn't show up today.*

- *I have to win this tournament or people (family, friends) will think less of me.*

- *I have to get a good shot off the tee or I will be embarrassed.*

- *My customer loves golf and if I don't play well he may take his business elsewhere.*

- *I've mastered this game.*

- *That (whatever it was) shouldn't have happened.*

- *I've put so much time and money into this game that I have to be really good at it.*

These beliefs have in common a stated or implied "should," "have-to," "ought-to," or "need-to." When your beliefs are based in these attitudes rather than in WANTS you open the door to fear, hurt and anger. The first list, as compared to "wants," creates a judgmental situation – a situation in which you judge yourself as good or bad, right or wrong.

I encourage you to keep in mind what you want, rather than how you think your game "should" be. Look for solutions and ways to think and behave that will move you toward your goals rather than away from them.

If you do this, then you, your golf clubs, your playing partners, and those of us who live on golf courses will have much more enjoyable and safer rounds of golf.

Section III

Golf puts man's character on the anvil and his richest qualities – patience, poise and restraint – to the flame

- Billy Casper

A TRUST WALK

Ah, the Masters!

Ah, THE MASTERS!

Affectionately known in the golf world as the "Holy Grail of Golf," this is one experience that more than lives up to its mighty reputation. From the first step, walking under the famous white porticos, to watching the drop of the last winning putt, you are drenched in the history, tradition and mystique that is the game of golf.

It's all there.

The challenge of a spectacular course. The course is groomed to perfection and designed to require golfers to reach into the deep recesses of their skills, imagination and courage if they are to be victorious.

The players, challengers, chosen few. Fierce competitors all, each has the prerequisite skills to be a contender, to be a winner.

The fans. Known as the most knowledgeable gallery on the tour, they both look and act the part. As befits the South, there is a genteel quality to the crowd as they walk briskly in the morning to place their chairs in the perfect spot for the day's viewing. Even if unoccupied for several hours, a placed chair is respected and left to await its owner's return.

The tournament is steeped in a history and tradition that is made tangible by watching golf greats Gene Sarazan, Sam Snead, and Byron Nelson open the tournament with their honorary drives off the first tee, by standing under the huge umbrella tree in front of the clubhouse, or by viewing the memorabilia within the clubhouse. You know you are someplace very special.

Even the name, _The Masters,_ reminds us that golf at its best is always about personal mastery. Victory in golf is a personal victory; it is a melding of the physical, mental, emotional and spiritual aspects of self into a whole – a whole capable of successfully meeting the challenges that come before it during four days of rigorous competition. That is no small feat, especially at Augusta National.

In the 1998 tournament, no one could deny the electricity generated by U.S. Amateur Champion, Matt Kuchar, whose skill and infectious smile won the crowd over in short order. Starting his first round as a relative unknown, paired with Tiger Woods, he said he was a bit intimidated at first, but that Tiger helped put him at ease: "He was really helpful to me. He talked and joked and that made it easier. He went out of his way to help me relax."

It didn't hurt that the hearts of the large gallery following these two were quickly captured by this engaging gentleman from the University of Georgia who forever smiled, even after a double bogey. It was a love affair born of the delight of watching Kuchar truly enjoying the game of golf while playing at a highly competitive level.

And then there was the Golden Bear, Jack Nicklaus, thrilling the crowd as he sank birdie putts and made everyone believe that anything's possible.

If the winner was chosen by a popularity contest, it would have been close – with Nicklaus having a slight edge. Though all played well, the ultimate winner finally emerged from the pool of great players that lay between Kuchar and Nicklaus and the history they represented.

And "finally emerged" is the way to put it. Another tradition at The Masters is that the winner is usually unknown until the last few holes of play on Sunday. Tiger's domination in 1997 was a noteworthy exception. The 1998 tournament win by Mark O'Meara fit the mold.

The best way to win at Augusta is to have a game plan and stick with it through thick and thin. It is important to hold the belief that you're capable of winning while at the same time recognizing that you may not, and that either way, it is not a statement of your personal worth.

The concentration and the focus exhibited by the players was intense. The air around many players seemed almost brittle as they strode purposefully down fairways and onto greens.

In fact, it was remarkable when the entire field walked by a large group of spectators (seated on the grassy slope beneath the tee box of the par three number six), and only three of the players indicated an awareness of the crowd. Even though the crowd was cheering, clapping, and calling players' names, nearly all focused straight ahead, looked down, or remained engaged in conversation with their caddie. Nicklaus, Zoeller, and Kuchar were the exceptions. They waved, smiled, and made eye contact with the group of adoring fans. They made you especially glad you came.

Many of the players seemed to believe the myth that the "Hogan Way" is the only way. Ben Hogan is known for his intense concentration and his need to block out all distractions by becoming exceptionally introverted on the course. This worked for him, and it works for some others, perhaps like Nicklaus in his earlier years, but it doesn't work for everyone. In fact, if it is not natural to your temperament and personality, it can prevent you from playing at your best.

Watching the players brought to mind the "tension of trying," and the "got-to's" of grinding, versus the tranquility of trust – trusting yourself to find the right balance between "looking out" and "looking in" on the golf course. Finding the right balance for you is one of the mental skills that is beneficial to any golfer, whether pro or amateur.

I encourage you to experiment on the golf course. At times practice introversion, excluding all that is around you by the intense focus held within. Other times see what happens if you chat with your buddies, enjoy your surroundings and play more outside yourself. Also try some blending of the two, perhaps with the goal of being able to move in and out of intense focus for each shot. Know that your right balance will be unique just as your best swing is unique.

Believing in yourself and finding your own way to approach the game is a potent skill for all golfers. It leads to greater consistency and lower scores. Perhaps if more of the pros openly expressed their unique styles, an extraordinary golf event like The Masters would be even more pleasurable to watch.

The Masters, by its very nature, asks everyone involved to be at their very best. No one is immune from its spell – not the players, the spectators, the officials, the sponsors, the media, the groundskeepers or the multitude of volunteers. And certainly not the clean-up crews, who, decked out in their official bright yellow uniforms, unobtrusively and diligently pick up any piece of litter almost before it hits the ground.

It is a privilege to witness this class act, and easy to understand why tickets are carefully guarded and handed down from generation to generation. To paraphrase the song "Maria" from <u>West Side Story,</u> "The Masters" are two of the most beautiful words golfers round the world have ever heard.

> **"The Masters.** Say it loud and there's music playing.
> *The Masters.* Say it soft, and for golfers, it's almost like
> praying," as could only be true of the Holy Grail of Golf.

It's Easy When It's Easy

"**W**hen it's easy, it's easy," said Freddy Couples during the 2001 Phoenix Open at the TPC in Scottsdale, Arizona. Couples elaborated, "When it's hard, that's when the mental skills of the better players will set them apart from the rest of the pack." Almost anyone who plays golf would agree with that statement.

"When you're not playing well, not striking the ball well, is when you have to have a good mental day," explained Couples. "If you're playing poorly, mentally you have to be way above normal to get around. You can't throw away another shot, because the next day you may wake up and birdie three of the first five holes and end up shooting a 68."

"I don't hit the ball the way I used to," said Couples, "but when I do play well, I also think a lot better." He continued, "I don't play as many rounds in a season, but I think I'm actually better [mentally] on the course. You get young kids and they don't know about getting into tough situations. Thursday, Friday, Saturday – those drives are easy to hit, but come Sunday, you have to play into the golf course, not babying the ball around, but playing smart."

Couples has been around and with experience has come wisdom.

Couples joined the PGA Tour in 1980, and has 14 tour victories to his credit, including the 1992 Masters. Voted by his peers as PGA Tour Player of the Year in 1991 and 1992, he is also repeatedly voted one of the most popular players on tour by fans.

Though his last Tour wins came in 1998 at the Bob Hope Chrysler Classic and the Memorial Tournament, Couples stated emphatically,

"I don't do hindsight. You are what you are," he said. "Some days you play well and don't think well, and other days you think well but don't hit the ball well. The score can be the same on both days."

He seems to have learned acceptance. It would be helpful for all golfers to remember those words of wisdom and apply them to our games (and even to a season of golf).

Couples likes playing in Pro-Am events: "Some of the tournaments I've played best in are the Pro-ams, like the Bob Hope or in Vegas. You spend a lot of time by yourself, waiting on the other guys to hit. It's hard for some [professionals], like players in their 1st, 2nd, or 3rd years out here. They might get frustrated, but you do it all the time and you get used to it."

The hardest part for him? "I get a little bit frustrated when fans are disappointed when I can't sign everything everyone wants me to sign, and then they think I'm a bad guy." Watching Couples during the Xerox Silver Pro-Am on Wednesday at the Phoenix Open, he took time to sign many autographs, but the disappointed rumblings of those fans left with unsigned hats, programs, or badges could plainly be heard.

Think for a minute how much you want others to think well of you. Are you so concerned with what your playing partners think of you that you forget to focus on making your shot? If so, do what Couples said, "I just remember I can only do the best I can."

"I laugh because it sounds easier than it is," he said. And, with his smooth swing ,and amicable style, he makes it look really, really easy. But then, it is "easy when it's easy." Freddy Couples is also champion enough to even make it look easy even when it's hard.

Know Yourself – Play in the Present

Speculation was strong that Jack Nicklaus might be playing in his final U.S. Open when he competed at the 100th Open at Pebble Beach in 2001. Commentators reminded viewers of his many accomplishments and trophies as everyone watched him trudge along one fairway after another during his two rounds at Pebble. It was clearly not his finest hour on the golf course.

At the conclusion of his second round, interviewers asked about his experience in this tournament. Interviewers asked Nicklaus what he was thinking as he moved from hole to hole; they clearly wanted him to wax sentimental about the bygone years, and his longing for things past. This was, after all, what the media had been giving the viewing audience all day long.

Nicklaus, however, would have none of it.

Asked what he remembered most about past Opens as he strode around the course on this memorable day, Nicklaus answered: "I think that's something mostly the press pays attention to. It might have been good to do more remembering while I was out there but I was busy just playing each shot, trying to figure out what I wanted to do on each shot, not thinking about the past. I might have more time for that when I retire."

That's the reply of a champion, and the reason he has all those "glorious old days" to look back on, if he ever gets around to retiring. Which I hope he doesn't.

Golf, like life, is best played, enjoyed, and relished in the present moment. Play with the clear knowledge and intention that this present moment is the only one you have; it is the building block for whatever future you will create for yourself.

Every really good golfer will tell you that their ability to be patient and stay in the moment gives them success on the golf course. Being and staying fully present to the shot in front of you is the most demanding mental element found in the game. The process for staying "in the moment" is unique to each golfer.

One golfer may go through an elaborate pre-shot routine, and hold the target in mind fully emblazoned in technicolor. Another equally successful player may simply walk up to the ball, have a subtle swing key in their awareness, and pull the trigger. A third player might not have a routine of any kind, preferring to be totally spontaneous and do what "feels right" for each shot.

Each and every player will find their own way to stay in the moment, but the routines of successful golfers share a few essential elements. Those shared elements are:
1) A clear intention of what you want to achieve,
2) A *knowing* that you are capable of doing what is necessary to reach your goal, and
3) A clear image of the outcome before you produce it.

Ever notice how you seem to execute best for the toughest shots? Tough shots capture our attention more than so-called "easy" ones. On easy shots, you might walk up to the ball and just swing away, not taking time to assess all the factors, or make the shot interesting enough to hold your attention. It's important to make every shot interesting and be creative with each shot.

Once you have decided on the shot you want to make, it becomes an issue of whether you can execute that particular shot or not. *Knowing* is several steps beyond "thinking you can accomplish something." Knowing means *certainty*.

I'm sure you've had the experience of walking up to a putt or a full-swing shot and just knowing that you are going to put the ball exactly where you want it. Knowing is an internal state in which all aspects of you (body, mind, emotions, spirit) are on the same page.

Knowing is the result of practicing and honing your physical skills while persistently holding beliefs that are aligned with your highest values and which support movement toward your goals.

Now that you *know* you can execute the shot you want, take the time to imagine it happening just the way you want it. And remember, imagining is not just visualization. Imagery is a natural language for each of us and can be done with all or any of our senses. You might see the image, hear it, feel it, sense it or just know it. One player even said to me, "I can almost *taste* sweet victory."

Each of these mental skills happen in the moment and produce the focus, concentration and confidence that every golfer seeks.

Nicklaus is noted for the intensity of these traits on the course. And now Tiger Woods is noted for the same traits; he doesn't look back, he is intense in the present moment as he creates the future he *knows* will be his.

A TRUST WALK

A Man With a Secret

Mike McCullough is a man with a secret.

McCullough, who joined the PGA Tour in 1972, and the Senior PGA Tour in 1995, may have taken only second place in the 2001 Countrywide Tradition at Desert Mountain in Scottsdale, Arizona, but he has a lot of guys on tour wondering, "What is his secret?" And he's not telling.

Attention turned to McCullough in 2000 when he had his best tour season ever and became laser-like in 2001 with his wins at both the 2001 Mexico Senior Classic, and Emerald Coast Classic, a second place at the Tradition, and fifth place at the Siebel Classic in Silicon Valley.

All eyes turned questioningly to McCullough, wondering what he was doing differently and what magic he had learned. After all, this was the same guy who had played in 156 consecutive senior events without winning once.

Most people attribute his new-found success to his work with teaching pro Ernie Vossler, introduced to McCullough by his buddy, and fellow competitor, Gil Morgan. Even McCullough suggests that a new relationship with, and a new understanding of, his swing is contributing to the success: "The swing is illusive, I've learned more about what is supposed to happen."

McCullough described a telling experience which occurred at the last hole of the Emerald Coast Classic: "Coming into the last hole I knew if I birdied the hole I could win outright. I knew I needed to at least par the last hole. I had a five iron onto the green. As you get older those longer irons are more difficult. So, I set up, I was excited about trying to execute the shot, and I didn't pull it off."

He went on, "I immediately knew what didn't happen, and knew that if I could drop down another ball I would make a good correction. The Mike McCullough of old wouldn't have known what to do."

I asked, "The Mike McCullough of new, what did you do?" And that's when he acknowledged he had a secret: "Well, I don't tell people what I'm working on. But what I did was recognize the good things in the swing, and recognize what didn't take place, not being negative, but I just knew what didn't take place."

He continued, "I know what the ball needs to do. I know what I'm capable of doing with the ball, and I know how to change the ball flight. Once I start it into motion then it takes place, and if things in my body don't function properly, then it doesn't take place. And I know where to go for that next shot to make the correction. Very rarely have I been in that form before these last two years."

McCullough said, "I went from a 'feel' player to being more successful. I'm ball-flight oriented. If the ball flight functions properly then the target gets in the way."

Is that his secret? Maybe, maybe not.

McCullough went on to say, "I don't want to be measured for my victories. I want to be measured for what I do with my life, and if I'm blessed with chances to be recognized, I hope I made the proper decisions."

What's important to him? "The Lord and my family, that's it. If the Lord gives me success then I want to use it properly. I've had a fear of not doing the right thing. Money used to be a thing that I'd say, 'Gosh, I don't know if I can handle that I might become a material person.' Apparently He thinks I'm strong enough to handle it now, so we'll see."

60

"How's it going so far?" I asked him.

"I still feel like I have my first three nickels. I still feel like I know the value of a dollar. I'm not going to give Him the credit for winning or losing; I don't believe he does that. I believe He gives you the opportunities. He gives you the abilities and you use them yourself. I hope I use my abilities properly. I need a lot of support from Him; He really needs to lean on me. I'm far from being who He wants me to be."

"You've got to be content with yourself, and make mistakes and correct them. Be willing to love yourself. You have to love yourself before you can love your neighbor. My wife, my children, we're on the same page."

Now, YOU decide: What is his secret?

A TRUST WALK

Get to Know the Kid

There's a new kid on the block. He moved into our minds and hearts during the 81st PGA Championship at Medinah Country Club, and he adds a lot of class to the neighborhood. Watching him we were awed and reduced to giggles. He scampered, leapt, gave high-fives and grins; he invited each and every one of us to feel his feelings and visit his home of pure exuberance. You couldn't watch him play golf and not feel good about him and the game.

Sergio Garcia was the second youngest player to compete in the PGA Championship, and the youngest runner-up ever in PGA Championship history. And, at 19 years old, he exhibited and often described a formidable mental game as surely as he showed off his considerable prowess, finesse, and courage with a golf club. His "tree shot" on number 16, where he hit the golf ball while it was lying inside the roots of a tree, was a historic shot for the ages, and underlying that shot appears to be a mind for the ages as well.

Think about this for a moment: it's Sunday afternoon, the final round of the PGA Championship, you're two shots back of Tiger Woods and playing just ahead of him. Parring number one, you stride to the tee of number two, a gnarly par three with a water carry to a pin cut on the very left-hand edge. You dump it into the water, but go on to salvage a bogey from what could have been a disaster.

Following the tournament, when you're asked about the shot that ended in the water you reply: "Thanks for reminding me because I didn't remember I hit it in the water on the second. When you tell me about the water, I was – which hole was it? I just forgot it after I made the bogey putt; I forgot I hit it in the water."

HE FORGOT HE HIT IT IN THE WATER?!

Do you ever remember a time at the 19th hole when you or a playing partner *forgot* one that you put into the water? In fact, isn't it usually the opposite? Players bemoan the lousy shots they made, the bad breaks they got, and the "just missed" opportunities. The focus and greatest concentration of energy are put on what went wrong rather than what went right.

Not remembering the shot doesn't mean that Sergio is great at denial, or at blocking out things that are unpleasant to remember. It means that he is great at holding his attention where he wants it; he is great at choosing where he will focus, and where he will concentrate his energy.

You can add this mental skill to your game.

Before your next round decide to practice this skill. Score your ability to focus, direct your energy and maintain your concentration. Make yourself a score card with blank spaces to write down what you notice about your focus and self-talk on each shot for every hole. Also notice what you remember after the round is over. Do you tend to remember the ones that got away, or do you remember the great shots? Or both?

The point of this exercise is to just notice what is present. Do not try to change anything, just notice what you do and how you do it. Where is your attention placed? Are there patterns to what happens? Does your focus or self-talk change after a missed shot? After a couple of missed shots in a row? Do the wheels come off? Do you climb on the bogey train? How do you re-tighten the lug nuts? Get off the train?

We can consciously choose only those things of which we are aware, so learn about yourself. Notice as much as you can about what you say, think and do on the course, and ask yourself if it takes you toward your goal, or away from it. And remember, what works and doesn't work will be unique to you.

Through self-awareness you can grow in your ability to actively choose your focus, the mental habit that serves the pros and other top players so well.

When you can choose your focus, you increase the chance that, like Sergio, you can turn dreams into reality. Sergio was asked about his eventful year and what he was feeling after finishing runner-up in the championship. He was asked if his finish surpassed his expectations.

His response? "I was dreaming about that, not expecting. It was one of my dreams for this year...play The Masters as an amateur, then turn pro, try to do well, win my first tournament this year and get on the Ryder Cup Team. But I knew it was difficult; I was very young and, well, there's a lot of great players around there. I've played well some tournaments, but I haven't done anything yet to be...somebody incredible or over some other players. I had four good tournaments, but still a long career to come and that's when I have to prove that I'm something else."

These are not the words of someone looking back; they are the words of a young man taking stock of his new "neighborhood" and dreaming of possibilities and then staying focused and building the home he wants.

A TRUST WALK

What Tiger Knows

Tiger Woods doesn't just believe – he **knows**; as a result of his knowing he is the best golfer in the world.

Tiger exhibits mental clarity, an absolute knowing, about who he is, his capabilities, and what he will and will not do in any given circumstance. He totally trusts himself on the golf course and it shows in his performance.

Remember the law of cause and effect: to create any desired effect learn the cause(s) and repeat them until the desired effect is obtained. If the effect you desire on the golf course is to play in a state of trust, then you need to understand what causes that state.

Trust results when you are in total accord within yourself mentally, emotionally, physically, and spiritually, and are aligned with your highest values.

You might be asking, "What does it mean to be emotionally, mentally, physically, and spiritually in accord within yourself?"

Let me explain. To begin:

YOU WILL NEVER HAVE EXACTLY THE SAME GOLF SHOT TWICE!

To approach each shot during a round of a golf as the "only shot" means you have a new beginning each time you walk up to the ball. This is a gift because you have an opportunity to choose what and how you think about the shot, what you believe, and thus how you feel about the shot. You get to decide what meaning you are going to give to each shot, and create the swing that will produce the shot you want to make.

The challenge is the challenge of "will." Using your willpower to consciously and actively choose to pay attention to each and every shot during a round of golf is a stumbling block for most players, even the pros. Tiger is the best I've ever seen at not only playing "one shot at a time," but also at using his will to creatively confront the unique challenge of each shot he makes.

In terms of confidence, Tiger has brought unparalleled innate physical and mental skills to the game, and through practice he has further honed his innate abilities to the razor sharpness you witness today. And yet, even with his skill, he must play one shot at a time, and be fully committed to that one shot, if he is to score his best.

There exists a "continuum of commitment to action," and Tiger is head and shoulders above most players in his commitment to a certain and specific action.

The continuum looks like this:

Know I am not	Believe I will not	Can't	Might	Should, ought to or need to	Want to	Will try	Can	Believe I will	Know I am

As Tiger stands over a shot, be it a 350-yard drive or a three-foot putt, his commitment to action is almost always of the variety that states; "I know exactly the shot to make in this situation (mental); I feel the sensations of confidence inside (emotional); I know the meaning I give to this shot is aligned with my highest values (spiritual); I know how to make this shot (physical)."

Where are you on the continuum of commitment to action? What do you experience inside yourself as you stand over a shot? If your inner experience is a sense of, "I know I am able," or "I believe I will," your chances of success are much greater than if your internal message is one of, "I'll try," or "I should," or "I want to," etc.

What does it take to reach this level of trust? To play "in the zone" as often as possible? To be in a state of "inner accord?"

- Practice (both the physical and the mental parts of the game)
- Persistence
- Clarity about your values and the meaning of golf in your life
- Self - awareness – what works for you and what does not
- The willingness to actively make decisions and choices – volition
- Imagination – the ability to use your skills in a creative manner

You might say that you can only reach this state of trust if you are Tiger Woods, but I would argue that you can feel trust in yourself regardless of your skill level. Trust is the product of self-awareness: know what you will and will not do; know your skill level and trust what is there; give golf the proper place in your life relative to your values, and play to the strengths in your physical game.

You will never <u>be</u> Tiger, but you might feel like a tiger on the course if you know who you are and play to your strengths!

A TRUST WALK

What is "IT?"

"IT" was on everyone's mind and everyone's tongue at the Olympic Club during the 1998 U.S. Open Championship. The spectators, media and players repeatedly speculated about IT.

Who had it? Who'd find it? Who'd lose it? Who had developed it? Who would hide it? Who would show it? Who could hold on to it? Especially during the stress of the final day and the final round on this most challenging of courses?

They wondered aloud about Payne Stewart: did he have IT in him to go wire to wire again and win another U.S. Open Championship? What was "it"?

MENTAL TOUGHNESS.

Everyone said this was the key to unlock the door to success and whichever player had this key on their key ring would emerge victorious.

Well, Payne Stewart didn't win, but does that mean he wasn't mentally tough? Or that he didn't have the most important ingredient of a winner? Did it mean that Lee Janzen, that year's U.S. Open Champion, had it while Stewart and the other players did not?

I don't think so. And I don't think Payne Stewart thought so either.

His words were the words of a mentally tough player:

"If you think well enough, and realize that you don't have your 'A' game that day then you do the best with what you have. This is learned deal – getting something positive from the bad situations. It takes a lot of mental toughness to be able to do that. If you let a pressure situation change your routine, then you don't have control."

And his actions were the actions of a mentally tough player.

Mentally tough people actively choose where they put their attention; they know that the object of their attention will be enhanced, in golf and in life. A pre-shot process is an example of directing and holding your attention where you want it. Stewart described his intentions: "What I do in my pre-shot routine, I make sure I do the same thing with each shot. I treat each shot the same, whether it's the first tee shot on Thursday or the last putt on Sunday."

He held to his routine throughout the final round, down to the last putt – a birdie putt opportunity on number 18 to tie Janzen and force a play-off. He treated that putt like every other putt; his process remained the same! He made a solid stroke, but the ball slid by. No playoff.

The game of golf is like life: you can do everything really well and still not always win. In fact you can do everything really well and not be the Champion. So what is mental toughness then?

Mentally tough people hold a belief about themselves, others, and the world in general in which success does not necessarily equate with winning. Mentally tough people know that expressing the best of themselves in each moment of life is what really counts.

Stewart expressed this toughness when he said, "I realize that my time is coming. I really believe that. I'm seeing a lot of positive things out there. It's a matter of one of these weeks I'm going to click and they're gonna be watching me."

Stewart saw himself as waiting to win again. Holding this belief gave him feelings of confidence, trust, flow, calm and peace. Just think what those feelings did for his golf swing. Even better, you could watch his golf swing, and see the effect of those feelings for yourself. Payne Stewart was known for his fluid, sweet swing.

Mental toughness is also about staying in the game and giving yourself every opportunity to win. It means being aware of your "self," and what works for you and what doesn't. As Stewart said, "Everybody's an individual and does different things to be mentally tough."

For Payne Stewart maybe that meant wearing knickers when no one else did. For Jim Furyk it's trusting his golf swing in all its uniqueness, and for Bruce Lietzke it's never practicing, because that's what works for him.

You may be thinking, "He was mentally tough and he still lost! Why did he lose?" The answer is one of the key beliefs that every golfer needs in order to make it out there, and Stewart said it well: "I lost because I didn't play well enough to win, and I was beaten by a great round of golf."

I also think he lost because golf, like life, is a very fickle game. Sometimes golf balls fall out of trees and sometimes they don't.

Payne Stewart may not have won the 1998 U.S. Open Championship, but he did give us a good example of the mental toughness necessary to put yourself in position to win. He taught us what we need to do out there to give ourselves that same opportunity to succeed: know and believe in your "self." Use your imagination and creativity to put your attention where you want it. Express the highest and best of who you are–even when it does not agree with conventional wisdom.

That's "IT!"

A TRUST WALK

The Mind of "Mrs. 59"

There's no question – golf is being played at a new level of excellence, and Annika Sorenstam is one of the players leading the way into the future. Records are falling almost every week, and a landslide occurred at the 2001 Standard Register Ping at Moon Valley Country Club in Phoenix when Sorenstam's second round score of 59 was posted.

That 59 crashed down like a huge boulder on the LPGA record of lowest score for 18 holes, and lowest score for 36 consecutive holes, while her 13 birdies in one round broke the previous mark of 11, and the score of 28 on her first nine holes broke a Moon Valley record.

Dubbed "Mrs. 59," Sorenstam, only one of four golfers in history (and the only woman) to score 59, went on to win the Standard Register Ping Tournament and flattened a final record with the win–she now held the record for the lowest score for any 72-hole LPGA event.

Sorenstam's mental toughness was impressive throughout the week, it was clearly the product of both her innate mental abilities, and the holistic training she received as a participant in the Swedish National Golf program from 1987-1992 under the tutelage of golf coach Pia Nilsson.

Speaking after the tournament, Nilsson described Sorenstam's natural abilities: "She is, and always has been, exceptionally stubborn and determined. Stubborn in a positive sense of knowing what she wants and sticking to it. It was in her. But there are so few players who dare to let themselves go and bring it out."

Sorenstam echoed Nilsson, saying, "I've set goals really high. I know what I want, and nothing is going to stop me. I think that's what is pushing me forward every day. I'm very stubborn. I want to be the number one player on the LPGA tour."

Nilsson continued her praise for the innate mental toughness possessed by Sorenstam: "She's willing to do what it takes to reach her goals. Annika is totally honest with herself about her weaknesses, and most important, she is willing to take the actions necessary to correct them. If there's an area to work on she takes action. She works hard, and she loves it. She loves the challenge. She doesn't blame outside forces; she looks to herself to be the best."

Nilsson described the philosophy of the Swedish Golf Federation program as, "an integration of the physical with being your best self mentally, emotionally, and socially." She continued, "We want our golfers to sort out who they are and what works best for them. We encourage them to create a life on tour that works for them, that supports who they are and what their goals are."

"We also believe we can shoot 54," said Nilsson. "And you have to start to believe in something before you can do it."

I would say Annika Sorenstam is definitely a believer: She *knows* she can shoot 54. Her friend, and LPGA tour player, Stephanie Croce seems to agree: "She always tells me she wants to shoot a 54 one day. In her mind, she believes she can make 18 birdies some day. The power of her mind is amazing. It's really what separates her from everyone out here. Talent is one thing, but Annika is something else. There are no doubts in her mind."

Following her round on Saturday, with Se Ri Pak hard on her heels, Sorenstam was feeling, not doubtful, but pretty exhausted: "I didn't sleep all night [Friday]. I was twisting and turning and thinking about my round and everything and when it came time to get up and come here and get ready, I was already tired. I felt like I had a hangover. I was exhausted from all the excitement and everything. I felt like I couldn't do anything this morning."

In spite of her fatigue, Sorenstam was able to hold off Pak by shooting a very respectable 69 to maintain a three-shot lead going into Sunday's final round. "When I look back on the round," said Sorenstam, "I'm very happy with the 69 because I didn't feel like I could do anything this morning. I felt like I was miles away from yesterday. But, you know, maybe it was to be expected."

Sorenstam said she was counting on getting a good night's sleep on Saturday, and she gave herself some added insurance by seeking out some additional support.

Sorenstam turned to Pia Nilsson for help in maximizing her own inner mental toughness. "She (Sorenstam) was still feeling a bit overwhelmed with all that had happened after the round on Friday. There was so much going on. It was hard for her to clear her mind and get focused on Sunday," said Nilsson of their conversation.

She went on to say, "Annika is exceptionally good at playing one stroke at a time. We talked more about how she could conserve her energy on Sunday. We discussed the importance of making a clear decision about each shot, and then executing that decision."

Nilsson said, "I told her, 'Even if you didn't sleep for a week, you have trained hard, your mind and body know what to do.' I reminded her: when you focus on each shot, one shot at a time, it's minutes, not hours, of concentration that is necessary. I helped her ...make it something she believed she could do in the midst of her mental and physical fatigue."

Sorenstam told Nilsson she knew she could do that. And she did.

They also talked about the importance of Sorenstam recognizing she could not control the final outcome, and making her peace with that. Sorenstam's words on Sunday, following her win, suggested the presence of just such inner peace to match her inner strength: "I'm so tired. I worked so hard this week. I focused on every single shot. It feels like I have been on the road for 10 weeks. If you had said someone would shoot 25-under and lose, [I] would have thought [you] were crazy."

But shooting 25-under and losing is exactly what happened to Se Ri Pak.

Sorenstam had a peaceful, satisfied look as she also acknowledged, "If someone beats you after you shoot 13-under, you just have to take hats off to them because that's incredible golf. You can't be unhappy with yourself. It comes to where you can't be disappointed with yourself. It was exciting. I never got nervous."

She added, "I wanted to win this tournament. If it was by 10 shots or 35, it doesn't matter. I just wanted to win."

And she had the mental toughness to make it so. Such is the power of the mind of "Mrs. 59." She made a believer out of me.

Sorenstam's performance clearly demonstrates that success in golf, or life, is not attained by singular focus on physical skills or possessing the right equipment. Success is built on a rock-solid foundation of mental, emotional, spiritual and physical clarity and well-being.

What about you and your game? What beliefs direct your actions on the golf course? Are you willing to honestly examine who you are, and your strengths and weaknesses? Are you willing to do whatever it takes to improve? If you are, then you, too, can reach for the moon and fulfill your goals. Maybe you can even be the first Mr., Ms. or Mrs. 54.

That's the power of your mind.

What Do I Want to Think?

What do I *want* to think right now?

That is the question that Scott Watkins, Director of Instruction at the Phoenician, said helped him win his fourth Southwest Section PGA Championship in September 1998 at Pinnacle Peak Country Club.

He won this same title in 1997 and in back-to-back victories in 1986-87. Scott sees himself as a better golfer now than at any time in the past, including when he was an All-American at Arizona State University, Pacific 10 Conference Champion, or a Tour player. He reflected on the differences in his current game:

"I think I'm smarter and I think my mechanics are better. I'm probably a more consistent putter. My weak point on the tour was putting. I used to leave it short all the time." "More important," he said, "I don't have the mental peaks and valleys as much as I did. I'm getting control of that."

How is he getting control of that? He described it this way:

"This year we played Pinnacle Peak Country Club, and their bent grass greens were really soft. We were required to wear soft spikes, and on those greens the spikes left pock-marks kind of like small craters. On the first day I teed off close to the end of the field and so the greens were pretty rough. For the first nine holes I got frustrated and a little upset every time one of those marks threw my putt off line. I was stroking the ball well, but still ended up with several three-putts. I was getting more and more tense inside; I wasn't having good luck."

79

Then things changed. No, the greens didn't suddenly, magically become smooth, but as Watkins said, "I thought about them differently. I accepted that they were just the way they were and that I couldn't do anything about it. I remembered that my only job was to put a good stroke on the ball. I was more at ease when I chose to think that way, and more putts began to fall. I ended up even for the day and knew I was in it."

"What I've learned," said Watkins, "is that when the anxiety begins to build, I want to take a step back and ask myself, 'What do you choose to think?' because what I am thinking is creating the anxiety."

What we tell ourselves, or how we interpret any given situation, will either move us closer or further away from our desired outcome. On the first 11 holes Watkins was thinking something like, "The greens shouldn't be this way." When he changed his interpretation to "the greens are just the way they are and everyone's playing them," he changed how he felt inside. He created a knowing that he had a chance to win. He knew he was in it!

As part of his pre-shot process, Watkins has learned to notice what is in his mind; he notes where his attention is in any given moment and literally asks himself the question: "Is this what I want to think right now? Is this what I want to pay attention to right now?"

"When I'm not playing well," he said, "I know that I"m not keeping my attention focused on my target. One of the first things that I notice is my eyes start wandering. Then I see something I don't like, trouble or something, and I say 'I don't want to go there.' "

Watkins went on to say, "The other thing that happens is that this feeling just pops into my head that I'm going to miss it left. I feel like Lee Trevino who said 'You can talk to a fade, but a hook won't listen.' On the 10th tee of the SWS Championship, it happened – that thought popped into my head. I might have been distracted by some folks talking on the nearby tee, but I didn't step back and go through my routine. I just went ahead and made the shot, and sure enough hooked it into the rough. I was allowing negative thoughts to be in control."

If he had remembered to step back and go through his pre-shot process, then he may have remembered to ask himself the question about his attention. If the answer was no, his attention was not where he wanted it, then he could ask, "What do I want to pay attention to right now?" He could then choose where to put his attention. In golf, he almost always wants his attention on the target.

"It really doesn't matter," he said, "what you thought 10 seconds ago; it matters what you're thinking about right when you're pulling the trigger, and that [question] kept me focused right at that point on what I wanted the shot to do, not what I didn't want it to do."

This routine made a difference. In the final round, Watkins came in at six under par with a 66 – a tie with the course record. That gave him a three-stroke margin of victory over Don Yrene, an assistant pro at Scottsdale's Gainey Ranch.

The mental skill that Watkins is describing is one that I call NOTICE AND CHOOSE. I encourage players to practice it on and off the golf course. For one day, each hour on the hour, notice where you are placing your attention. See what you discover about how you are using your energy. When we put our attention on something, we are fueling it with our energy. That is the creative process. The question to ask yourself is, "Am I creating what I want in my life with where I am placing my attention?"

Some golfers find it helpful to create a "trigger" or signal that will remind them to notice their thoughts and where they put their attention. A trigger works best if it is something that is a natural part of the golf experience. You give it special "powers" by simply designating it as your signal. For instance, you can decide that a particular head cover, golf glove, or even the tips of your shoes will be your signal. When you have made a commitment to that intention in your mind, then that object becomes the trigger or signal. It's not important what the trigger is, it's important that you make a commitment to the intention.

Scott Watkins had a great year, capping it off with being honored as the Player of the Year for the Southwest Section. Is he creating what he wants by where he places his attention? You bet he is.

"This feels pretty good," Watkins concluded. "I'm getting older and have less time to spend on my game than I used to. I've got three kids, and the youngest is six," he said, "and now is the time I need to be around." Scott has learned that actively choosing where and when he gives his attention allows him to balance all the aspects of his life in a way that creates success, and not just in golf.

Section IV

One of the most fascinating things about golf is how it reflects the cycle of life. No matter what you shoot, the next day you have to go back to the first tee and begin all over again and make yourself into something.

\- Peter Jacobsen

Play the Game

Golf is a _game_.

People _play_ golf.

The words _game_ and _play_ imply the intention to have _fun_. They speak of the possibility to experience pleasure in what you're doing out there on the golf course. In fact, almost every golfer I know says that one reason they play golf is to have fun and enjoy themselves and their friends on the course.

But you and I both know it's easier said than done. The fun is often elusive; the challenges and frustrations often seem to take what started out as a great walk in a beautiful place, doing something you enjoy, into the proverbial _good walk spoiled_.

So it was especially rewarding at the 2000 Phoenix Open, the PGA tour stop that's touted as "the place to be for a good time," to witness Tom Lehman, with his new-found commitment to having more fun with his golf game, show us something of how it's done.

Having more fun is a key goal for Lehman as he begins a new millennium of golf and seems to be an idea that helped him put his priorities into clear perspective. He said, "It's kind of been a common theme with me this week, trying to enjoy golf, to have fun, to enjoy playing. Same with putting. You know, good putters, they can't wait to get to the green; they can't wait to go ahead and try to make that putt."

He went on to describe his thinking and what he's doing to create more fun, "I've been trying to be way more right-brained with my putting, trying to just kind of let it happen almost. You know, I get on the putting green and I"ll putt, not thinking about anything but making the putt, and [I] make a lot of putts."

Part of the secret is being more childlike in his approach to the game. As Lehman said, "As a kid that's what you do...look at the putt, get the line, and then just kind of let instinct take over and just roll it up to the hole, as opposed to trying to force the ball in there. Just trying to get in that real loose, kind of instinctive feeling about putting."

Lehman's new theme was apparent right up to his winning putt on the 18th green: when it dropped into the cup, the kid within him pumped his fist emphatically into the air, exclaiming for all to see that he was indeed having the time of his life! The kid within made that final putt on the 18th, he stepped up, took dead aim, and rolled it in.

Later Lehman said, "Those are the same putts I've missed most of my career, so I was happy to step up and make it." His big smile left no doubt that he had fun on this Sunday afternoon and that he was happy with the success it brought him.

But sometimes "fun" isn't fun, or at least one person's idea of fun can be difficult for those around him. The Phoenix Open, with it's gaiety and rambunctious crowds, is also infamous as the place where some golfers find it difficult, if not impossible, to laugh with the crowds, especially if the crowd seems to be laughing at them.

David Duval had a hard time on Saturday; when he left the final hole to clean out his locker, he vowed not to return the next day because of the hecklers on the course. But he did return, and shot a 69 on Sunday. In my opinion that did more to quiet the hecklers than any rules or policies the Thunderbirds could endorse.

I like to think that Duval went home on Saturday, reflected on the day, and had the realization that those hecklers could not define him with their taunts, *they defined only themselves* as people who put others down as a way of trying to build themselves up.

I like to imagine that Duval recognized that the rude remarks were only about him if he allowed them to be, and gave his consent to be hurt by the comments of strangers. He discovered he had a choice. He could not stop the harassmeant, (and neither can the Thunderbirds or security unless the person breaks a law), but he could hold on to his personal power.

Duval could answer any of the following questions in a healthy way and take himself out of their grasp. Why, he might even have some fun denying them control of his life and experience.

"How am I going to think about this situation?"

"What do I want to believe right now?"

"What do I want to tell myself right now?"

"How can I create more pleasure for myself right now?"

In my imagination Duval learned a lesson that Tom Lehman seems to have figured out: if we change how we think, that changes how we feel, and if we change how we feel, that changes what we do. The one thing that no one can take away from us is our ability to think whatever we want to think. And that means we can put the "playing" back in golf.

When we think that fun and pleasure are part of playing the game of golf, even in the pro ranks where "playing" golf is a job, the correlation remains true: as the fun goes up – the scores go down, and vice versa.

A TRUST WALK

You Can't Fool Mother Nature

One of the reasons golf is so popular is it gives people an excuse to spend four-plus hours amidst the manicured beauty of Mother Nature. And yet, to their golfing peril, most golfers ignore some of nature's most defining truths even while basking in her glow.

The universe we live in is not governed by chance, it is governed by laws, and you can experience these laws of nature in action every time you tee up the ball. Let's take a look at three of mother nature's laws that have great impact on your game:

I.   _THE LAW OF CAUSE AND EFFECT_

II.   _THE LAW OF AVERAGES_

III.   _THE CYCLE OF PERFORMANCE_

I. The first law was put forth by Socrates more than 2000 years ago. He called it, _The Law of Causality;_ we now call it, _The Law of Cause and Effect._ This is both a mental and a physical law, and is often known as the "Iron Law of Destiny" for it's ability to imprison us in a cell of our own making, or free us to create experiences in line with our highest desires.

This law states that for every effect there is a specific cause. If you desire more of any given effect (like successful golf shots), then trace back to the causes for that result; repeat those exact causes and you will get the same results, or effects.

I'm sure you know plenty of golfers who grumble about their play while they do, say and think the same things, over and over again, and then are amazed they get the same results day after day.

A pre-shot routine can be an example of using the law of cause and effect to a positive advantage in your game, because it provides a process that incorporates mental, physical, emotional, and spiritual elements (all four being primary causes) that create the shot you want to make.

However, that same pre-shot routine, if it contains elements that take you away from being the best of who you are, will just as quickly take you to a poor outcome or a mis-hit golf shot.

Look for repeated patterns in what you think, say, do, and imagine on the course, and ask yourself if these various "causes" are giving you the shot-making effects you want.

If not, change the causes and look for new results. Sometimes you have to experiment with your self-talk, attention, beliefs, swing, or imagination to get the results you want. One of the reasons to seek out either a swing coach or a mental skills coach like myself, is to help you determine the best and most efficient way to experiment and get results faster than you could on your own. When you find the right combination, trust yourself, knowing that what works well for you will be unique from what may work well for your playing partners.

II. Your beliefs are the cornerstone of your emotional and physical life. They lead you to make certain interpretations about every experience you have on the golf course. It is important to understand the second law of nature, *The Law Of Averages,* so as to make interpretations that will be helpful to you on the course.

The law of averages tells you that every round of golf will contain a few great shots, a few poor shots, and a lot of what, for you, are average shots. However, that is not what most golfers seem to believe, nor is it how they react to any one golf shot, especially a bad one!

When golfers hit a poor shot, they often interpret that one shot as a defining moment for their entire round and say to themselves something like, "Oh no, the wheels are coming off," or, "There goes the round."

The next time you hit an errant shot, remember that every round will have a few of those, and remind yourself you've just gotten rid of one of them. Because of the law of averages, you have just *increased, rather than decreased,* the chance that your next shot will be of average or higher quality.

When you know this law of nature, your self-talk becomes more positive, with thoughts like, "It's bound to get better from here," or, "Glad I got that one out of the way," or "That's just one out of 80 (or whatever your average score might be), and my chances just improved!"

Remember that your thoughts are, quite literally, creative in nature.

III. Have you ever noticed player scores for any four-day professional golf tournament always seem to include three good scores and one not-as-good score? Or, in one of your rounds, or even the professionals' single round of play, have you noticed there are periods when you feel out of sync, and periods when you feel you can't miss?

If so, you have been noticing the third of Mother Nature's laws, the Law of Performance Cycles. As there are seasons in nature, and seasons to a person's life, there are seasons to golf performance, in each round, each multi-day tournament, and each year of golf.

A MAP OF THE PERFORMANCE CYCLE:

The Cycle of Golf ™

The Zone

Beliefs -
Feelings -
Behaviors -
Trusting Environment

"TRUST"

In Sync
Trusting

Out of Sync
Trying
(I Lost It!)
Wheels Coming Off

Begin
Play

"Trying Harder"

Letting
Go

Choosing
Physical
Self Talk
Imagery
Present Time
Expectations/Meaning

Noticing
Physical
Left Brain-Self Talk
Right Brain-Imagery
Meaning/Expectations
(Past & Future OR Present)

Clear Mind

When golf pros speak of patience, they are referring to the fact that getting "out of sync" is a natural and normal part of the cycle of performance; it is to be expected to show up at some point in each round. They have learned from experience that it is best to be patient, and trust that the cycle will come back around. They keep doing what they know works best for them, stick to their game plan, and simply wait it out. Such an approach gives them the best chance of allowing the cycle of performance to work for them.

Knowing about the natural cycle of performance means you will be more likely to trust it's natural movement rather than interfering by "trying too hard," and causing yourself to get stuck in the out of sync place within the cycle. Trust moves you around the cycle, while "trying" inappropriately can cause you to get stuck.

Getting too angry, deciding the wheels have come off, giving up, or feeling disgusted with yourself, are but a few of the ways to stick your feet in the mud of self-doubt and stop your progress around the cycle. Instead, stay patient, keep playing your game, and trust the cycle of performance to carry you around to being back in sync.

This may be a tough assignment for some of you, as it feels like letting go of "control" over your game. In reality this is a way to greater mastery, which is the ultimate achievement for any athlete. Mastery is about playing in congruence with the laws of nature, and trusting yourself to perform at your highest and best in accordance with those laws. Control is about trying, is counter to natural laws, and will not produce the best results.

Golf courses are beautiful and serene, and contain all the laws of nature within their boundaries. Remember, you can't fool Mother Nature, and it would be wise to play by her rules. You might even find yourself having more fun and achieving lower scores.

A TRUST WALK

It's Not Fair!

- Your golf ball hits a sprinkler head and bounds over the green leaving a difficult chip shot.
- A sudden gust of wind captures your ball and carries it several yards too far, or drops it like a hundred-pound rock short of your target.
- You make a good read, put a great stroke on the ball, and still it lips out of the cup.
- Your swing today is less rhythmic than other days.
- In the club championship you find yourself paired with the guy who talks incessantly, and you prefer quiet.
- On the day of the big tournament you get paired with the slowest player in the field, and you are the fastest (or vice versa).
- It starts to rain on the fifth hole of your round, and most of the other competitors are already in the clubhouse.
- Your ball lands in the fairway and mysteriously disappears – never to be found.

If you're like me, you probably think these examples show that golf is not *fair*. And you hate to admit it, but **you probably think it *should be* fair.**

"Fair" implies a set of circumstances in which the treatment of each player is the same. Rules created to ensure fairness on the playing field do not hold up under scrutiny. Golf challenges you to accept the impossibility of making the game fair.

Tiger Woods played by the rules when he allowed (invited) spectators to move a five-hundred pound boulder from in front of his ball during the 1998 Phoenix Open. A few players and fans accused

Tiger of not *playing fair*. They said other players do not have a horde of spectators to move mountains, or boulders, for them.

When you think the game should be fair, and it is impossible to make it so, it sets up a situation in which you may find yourself becoming angry, frustrated, upset, withdrawn or sullen. Golfing in any one of these emotional states is less than a pleasure, and no doubt your score suffers as well.

About now you might be asking, "What choice do I have?"

The choice is to recognize that although golf is not fair, it is *just*.

To "do justice" means to give due appreciation, and to "do oneself justice" means to do something worthy of one's ability. Golf meters out justice by being responsive to what we bring to the game. It is important to think about what you bring to the physical game and it is just as important to carefully choose what you bring to the game emotionally, mentally and spiritually (the spiritual component refers to the purpose and meaning you give to golf).

Golf promises challenges and obstacles for each player and seems to dare us to set foot on her playing fields. In the vast creativity of the game, no two golfers are confronted with the same exact challenges. The course seems to magically provide the situations each player needs to strengthen weak areas of his or her game and life.

And so a quiet golfer with solid swing mechanics is paired with "talkative Joe," thus challenging Mr. Quiet to mentally handle the situation. Meanwhile, his mentally tough playing partner can't seem to keep his tee shot in the fairway, requiring him to develop more skillful mechanics.

Golf courses are just there waiting for us to play them; they are perfect just as they are. The environmental conditions surrounding play are also "just what they are." They are not inherently good, bad, right or wrong. The golf course gives due appreciation when you do something worthy of your ability.

Your job is to bring the highest and best of you to the golf experience. That means *thinking, saying, doing* and *imagining* those things that consistently move you toward your desires rather than away from them. If you do that, golf will be *just* with you – it will be responsive to what you bring. Bring your best and you will experience the greatest pleasure and lowest possible score, for that day, on that particular golf course.

Golf is not fair, but it is just – even justified – in the difficulties it presents each player; golf encourages you to grow and respond in new, more skillful, and healthy ways. But don't take my word for it. Do yourself justice: pay attention when you and your partners play, and see if what I suggest holds true in your experience.

A TRUST WALK

Patience Makes Perfect

You know about patience.

Patience is a virtue.
Patience makes perfect.
Patience: use it or lose it.
It's the old joke: *I want it and I want it NOW!*

Tour players will tell you that patience can be your best friend, and lack of it your worst enemy. Jim Furyk, who said that patience is a key to success in the game of golf, was joined by Fuzzy Zoeller and Lee Janzen in extolling the virtues of developing this quality.

When asked what it was like to have so many putts "burn the rim" during his third round at the 1999 Phoenix Open, Furyk replied, "Patience is the most important [mental] thing out there." Furyk, the winner of five Tour events, including the 2000 Doral Ryder Open, continued, "The hardest part is being patient, just letting it happen. A lot of times you try too hard and get in your own way. You want to force the ball in the hole and you make more mistakes than if you just ride it out and wait for the momentum to go the other way. It's hard to just let things happen."

Patience is about letting things happen.

Fuzzy Zoeller, a crowd favorite with 10 Tour victories, echoed these sentiments when he said, "The main thing out here is not to lose patience. I mean, you're not going to play well every week, there're going to be weeks out here when you can't hit the old cow with a bass fiddle. Patience, to me, is hard to learn, but it's the one thing that's helped me a lot."

What about patience, Janzen style? He says, "No matter how I'm playing, I know that if I'm patient anything can happen, and certainly it only takes one good shot to get you going. You need to create an attitude before you go out, and maybe make up a set of [personal] rules or beliefs. I just realize that all the bad shots I've hit out there haven't ruined my life, so if I hit more bad shots I'll get over them. The more good experiences you have the better. You have to have a short memory in some instances [for the poor shots], and a long memory in others."

Furyk and Zoeller also point to experience as the best teacher of patience:

"It's hard to be patient and...work out of it by yourself," said Furyk. "It's hard for everyone. The older I've gotten the more patient I've become. It's a game of experience. That's why the average rookie is over 30 (years of age)."

"I think [patience] is more experience than anything," said Zoeller. "You go out and bogey one, or the first couple of holes, and most amateur golfers, their day would be ruined. With the pros, it's just two out of 18 because we have the ability to go out and catch a break, to make three or four birdies in a row. It's all self-confidence; it all comes down to that."

Okay, so you are not born with patience – it is something that you learn, create, or develop over time, with experience. And yet, what is it that experience provides that actually leads to patience?

Experience is the vehicle in which we use the four basic mental skills (self-awareness, beliefs, focus, and imagination), to develop greater patience. Even if you're the "grip it and rip it" type you can develop greater patience. Just look at John Daly, winner of the 1995 British Open, this is exactly what he has been learning for the past several years.

What is patience? It is being in the present moment and accepting that moment as perfect, just as it is. It is fully trusting yourself to be capable of creatively handling whatever comes your way in the next moment, while acknowledging that no moment is under your full control.

Furyk, Janzen and Zoeller, along with most professional golfers, male or female, use their experience as a way to get to know themselves. They discover what works for them, honor their unique qualities, and trust themselves explicitly.

These golfers have the experience to know how and what to tell themselves in a given situation to move toward their goals rather than away from them. They choose beliefs that support their personal goals.

Through experience they have practiced actively choosing where they want to put their attention and then putting it there and keeping it there through choice. They have practiced this skill until it became an unconscious habit they could trust.

And finally, experience taught them to rely on their imagination to creatively and effectively respond to an endless variety of situations – to trust that they will, more often than not, come up with a solution for even the trickiest of situations, or shots.

It all adds up to patience.

(Self-awareness + Beliefs + Focus + Imagination) x Experience = PATIENCE

Want more patience? Put youself in the above equation and let experience move you toward greater patience. And watch your scores drop in the process.

A TRUST WALK

Problems? Opportunities!

Golf is the most creative sport I know. Each time you step up to the ball a new adventure awaits you – a new opportunity to create a shot in the prevailing conditions. No two shots in golf are exactly the same, and every moment on the course provides an opportunity to be the most creative you can be.

You stop playing at your best when you stop bringing creativity to each shot. Many players say they get their best results when they are confronted with difficult shots – behind a tree, from the sand, a precarious lie–but mis-hits happen with easy shots – middle of the fairway with a good lie. Why? Because a shot defined as difficult gets your attention (and your creative juices flowing) more than does a simple, straight-forward shot.

The key is to approach each shot as a creative opportunity – a creative problem to be solved. Make easy shots more interesting by choosing a very specific target that is tougher to hit, or imagine more fully the "exact" shot you want, and see how close you can come to replicating it.

If golf shots are viewed as problems to be solved, it is helpful to define "problem" in the right way. John Maxwell, a motivational speaker, gives the following definition of problem and thus provides a way to think about golf shots as problems to be solved creatively:

P   stands for predictor: How you handle problems predicts much about your life experience. It's like the old saying: "It's not what comes into your life that matters, it's how you think about what comes into your life that defines who you are and the life you will live."

R   stands for reminder: Problems serve as a reminder that life will always have challenges. No matter how well you live, how well you choose, how much you do right, you will still be confronted with problems – with creative opportunities.

O   stands for opportunity: A problem is an opportunity for you to create a solution which reflects the highest and best of who you are mentally, emotionally, physically and spiritually.

B   stands for blessing: Blessings are experiences which teach you about yourself and the world and allow you to live a more meaningful and fulfilled life.

L   stands for lesson: Personal growth usually comes gift-wrapped in the gilded box of a problem. Problems provide lessons for living and playing.

E   stands for everywhere: Problems are everywhere, and everyone has them. That is how life and golf are designed, and what makes each interesting and challenging.

M   stands for messages: Just like the indicator lights on the dashboard of your car, problems are messengers, grabbing your attention and requesting or demanding that you take action and create a solution.

S   stands for solvable: Every problem has a solution. It may take everything you have to confront a particular problem, and none of the solutions may seem ideal, but you always have options and choices available to you. You have at least three broad choices:

1) You can leave; go away; get away. (As Snoopy said, "There's no problem too big to run away from.") 2) You can give up and leave the decision to others, or to the forces of nature that surround you. (To **not** choose is to choose.) 3) You can take whatever time and resources necessary to creatively experiment with alternatives until you find an answer that is the best possible one for that particular time and place in your life (or game).

I'm talking about attitudes, beliefs and intention. These are some of the tools necessary for creative golf. They are mental tools you choose to carry with you on the course. Just like you pick clubs best suited to your body and swing, you choose mental attitudes and beliefs that best fit your personal worldview.

We all know people who are pessimists, and we all know people who are optimists – which are you? Do you believe attitude is a choice? Do you practice choosing your attitudes? Do you practice choosing your beliefs about problems and challenges?

The next time you go to the golf course take note of your personal approach to each shot. Do you see it as a solvable problem and a creative challenge? If not, how do you approach each shot? Learn from what you notice, and choose the approach that works best for you.

In creative golf, each tee box is a new beginning, an empty canvas upon which you are able to paint a portrait of you at your highest and best. The gift is that it's never too late to do well, unless you give up and quit. Failure happens only when you quit, and regrets result only when you don't take the risk of bringing your creative juices to the game.

Remember, every miracle is borne of a problem.

Stress That Strengthens

STRESS has gotten a bum rap – the good lumped in with the bad. The fact is, you want stress in your life. If all the stress were gone from your life, death would be the result. If you are alive, stress is part of your life – it is everywhere all the time. It is unescapable.

The trick is to understand stress and use it to benefit your life rather than be harmful. There is stress that weakens, and stress that strengthens. "Stress Management" decreases the unhealthy stress and increases healthy stress.

Rather than ask, "How do I get rid of stress?" ask, "How do I create stress that makes me a better person?"

Stress is the effect of life energy in action. Actions are expressed in word, thought, imagination, and behavior. The goal is to intentionally create positive stress by expressing your life energy in actions that promote health and well-being.

Actions reflecting personal choice and responsibility create positive stress. Actions born of fear, called reactions, create unhealthy stress.

Take putting for example. Rather than saying:

"I have to make a birdie."
"I need to make a birdie."
"I should make a birdie on this hole."

You could say:

"I will make a birdie on this hole."

"I am capable of making a birdie on this hole."
"I want to make a birdie on this hole."
"I know how to make a birdies, I have practiced, and I putt well."

Your body has bio-chemical responses to your actions. This creates positive or negative effects, called stress, that are experienced as inner feelings and sensations.

Look for these qualities in stressors (actions) that strengthen:

1. You believe the actions are healthy for you.
2. The actions create positive sensations within you such as, peace, joy, anticipation, desire or excitement.
3. There is a feeling of courage or confidence present during your action.
4. The action is meaningful in your life and fits your value system.
5. The action requires you to develop, grow, or maintain a positive aspect of yourself. This aspect can be mental, emotional, physical, spiritual or any combination of these.
6. Your action is not a reaction to fear; it is a step toward what you want for your life.

So, go ahead – stress yourself to the MAX and to your maximum strength!

Anatomy of a Ten

Once when Arnold Palmer took a twelve on a hole, a writer asked him,"How did *you* get a twelve on that hole?"

Arnold in his humble manner, replied, "Well, I had a three-foot putt for an eleven, and I missed it."

Sometimes the shots seem to add up like they have a life of their own, multiplying like rabbits when you're not looking. Sometimes it's hard to add up all the shots needed to get that little white ball in the cup safe and sound. This experience is especially disheartening during a tournament or when you want to impress your boss or best friend. But most players, including the professionals, have had the experience more than once on the course. Even Tiger Woods has taken a double digit on occasion.

Because it happens to all of us, I thought it might be interesting and educational to look at "the anatomy of a ten." *Mine.*

No, not *that* anatomy and not *that* 10. I'm going to explore in detail how you (and I) end up with a double-digit score on a single hole. Not surprisingly, I will focus on the mental errors that come into play.

Let me describe my experience at the Dunes Golf and Beach Club in Myrtle Beach, South Carolina. One of the best known courses in the world, the Dunes has hosted five Senior Tour Championships, the Women's US Open, and the PGA Tour Q-School; it was named one of "America's 100 Best Classical Courses," by *GolfWeek/Golf & Travel* (1997-1999).

For me, the course was summed up by the sign which read "Waterloo," on the 13th hole. That sign describes the experience of many golfers on this hole. It is a dog-leg right, par five that is rated America's 4th best par 5 by *Golf Digest* (1999). Best. Worst. Sometimes they're the same thing.

A little background to set the stage for this adventure: the 47th Annual *Golf Writers Association of America* Championship took place in Myrtle Beach, and I was participating for the first time. Out of a field of approximately 150 players, there were four women. Not only did I have the pressure of being a sports psychologist in the midst of this den of mental thieves, I had the enormous weight of being a *female* sports psychologist. You can only begin to imagine the jokes.

The second day of the tournament was played at the Dunes, where, as of September 1999, caddies had returned to carry bags and help players read the undulating, quick-breaking, slick greens. For our tournament we had one caddie for each foursome; he was responsible for locating balls, providing yardage, raking bunkers and keeping up the morale of the players. Our caddie was also a pretty decent sports psychologist.

My foursome teed off on number 10, and I'm pleased to report that my tee shot split the middle of the fairway. I was just short of the green on my second shot, made an okay chip, and two-putted for an acceptable bogey. Holes eleven and twelve were unremarkable; I parred one and bogeyed the next. I didn't realize what lay ahead of me at the infamous thirteenth hole.

My eyes were first captured by the signs which read: "Watch for Alligators." As if that were not enough, my fellow, and I mean *fellow*, playing partners walked me over to the tee box to show me a permanent plaque: the plaque told of a GWAA player who had taken a twenty-two on this hole without ever hitting the water.

A twenty-two! And without going in the water!

Well, in my best sports psychologist manner, I decided that his experience had nothing to do with me; I would simply put my attention where I wanted it, keep my focus, play one shot at a time and escape humiliation and regrets.

Grabbing my driver from the bag, I looked down the fairway, chose a target on the right side, and let it rip! It was as beautiful a drive as I am capable of producing. I felt great. I strode down the fairway to my ball and began sizing up my lie, the wind, and the distance needed to carry across the water hazard and set up my approach shot to the green. Just then the caddie ambled over to my side, he looked at my ball, gazed out over the water, and pointed to the golf cart of the foursome in front of us. He said confidently, "That's where you want to aim."

After the players in the cart moved, I went through my pre-shot process, held my target clearly in mind, and took a relaxed swing. I made pretty good contact but faded the shot enough that it got wet. I took my drop, picked out the same target as before and held it in mind. I took an OK swing, hit it a bit fat and put that one in the water too. Now I was laying five and as I took the ball thrown to me by my partner, he chuckled and said, "This is the last one I have; if you miss it you have to walk back to the cart for another one."

This time I picked my own target – one in which I felt confidence. I kept the target in mind and let it fly. I put a good swing on it, held my breath and watched with relief and inner glee as it sailed over the water and landed in the distant fairway. I was there in SIX and when I walked to the cart I didn't have to come back this way.

At this point my partners decided to tell me that it is a tradition of GWAA to present a prize to the player with the highest score on this hole who still breaks a hundred. It was clear they thought I would be in the running. Mulling over this newest information, I walked to my ball for the approach shot to the green, which was still 160 yards away. Choosing a club, I picked out my target and held it in mind, but I was aware of a subtle image lurking in the corners of my mind: it was the image of me being called in front of 146 male golf writers and handed the "booby prize" for the tournament. I hit it fat and landed short. The image went from subtle to stark.

Laying seven, still off the green, I was looking at an uphill chip onto a slick, undulating green that breaks severely off to the right. (Don't you just love this game?) I stroked the ball well, too well, and hit it ten feet past the pin. Now I had an eight, and I was above the hole looking at a slick, curving putt for nine. I missed it on the high side and finally dropped a two-and-a-half foot putt for a final score of TEN. My partners wondered aloud if it would be enough to earn me the ignoble prize at the end of the tournament. We'll get back to that in a minute.

This is clearly an example of what not to do and a great opportunity to learn. The best you can do when things have not gone well is to ask yourself what you can learn from the experience so you do not repeat the same mistakes.

I learned the following: 1) as much as a good caddie knows, I have to trust the shot I'm about to make, 2) some images are very powerful, even if subtle; next time, rather than try to get rid of the image I will remind myself that images come to help, not hurt; they simply want to be listened to, not denied. All I needed now was a great one-liner to use at the dinner if it became necessary.

The end of the story? Someone else was good enough to take an eleven on number thirteen and still break 100, so when I was introduced to the group that night I was spared. And you will be, too, if no matter the anatomy of your Waterloo, you choose to learn from it.

My proudest moment at the Dunes was when I made par on the 14th hole.

A TRUST WALK